D1172538

THE DEVELOPMENT DILEMMA

The Development Dilemma

Security, Prosperity, and a Return to History

Robert H. Bates

PRINCETON UNIVERSITY PRESS

PRINCETON AND OXFORD

Published by Princeton University Press,
41 William Street, Princeton, New Jersey 08540

In the United Kingdom: Princeton University Press,
6 Oxford Street, Woodstock, Oxfordshire OX20 1TR

press.princeton.edu

Library of Congress Cataloging-in-Publication Data

Names: Bates, Robert H., author.
Title: The development dilemma : security, prosperity, and a return to history /
Robert H. Bates.
Description: Princeton : Princeton University Press, [2017] | Includes bibliographical
references and index.
Identifiers: LCCN 2017013209 | ISBN 9780691167350 (hardback : alk. paper)
Subjects: LCSH: Economic development. | Economic development—
History. | Economic history.
Classification: LCC HD78 .B37 2017 | DDC 338.9—dc23 LC record available at
https://lccn.loc.gov/2017013209

British Library Cataloging-in-Publication Data is available

This book has been composed in Adobe Text and Gotham

Printed on acid-free paper. ∞

Printed in the United States of America

10 9 8 7 6 5 4 3 2 1

To Elizabeth, Peter, Alexandra, and Laura

CONTENTS

ILLUSTRATIONS

Figures

Tables

PREFACE

I once served on the same faculty as Eleanor Searle and John Benton; they shared their knowledge of medieval history with me and in return I taught them about Africa. In keeping with the CalTech tradition, we taught each other by co-teaching students. In this, perhaps my last book, I return to the discussions we had before, after, and during those classes, seeking to make use of the materials to which they introduced me.

I wish to thank Philip Hoffman, Roger Noll, and Thayer Scudder, also of CalTech, and Jean-Laurent Rosenthal, Barry Weingast, Avner Greif, and Margaret Levi, with whom I worked on *Analytic Narratives*,[1] a project that also lay at the intersection between history and political economy. I also wish to thank Idriss Fofana, Kaiyang Huang, Georgia Stasinopolous, Alyssa Yamamoto, and Ethan Amaker—undergraduates at Harvard University—who gathered and analyzed data on the developing world, including the "lights data" on which I base my measure of regional inequality. I give special thanks to Didi Kuo, who directed their efforts. Kaiyang Huang assisted me in the collection of data on the formation of empires. Edem Fagbolagun assisted in the collection of data on urbanization in England and France. Ahsan Barkatulla provided superb assistance in the collection, cleaning, and analysis of data. Thanks, too, to Connor Jerzak for so ably stepping in when Ahsan later left for law school. Helen Ye Zhang scrutinized the manuscript for errors in spelling, dates, and other important details.

I produced the initial draft of this manuscript at the Russell Sage Foundation in New York during 2007–8; rewrote it at the Center for Democratic Development (CDD) and the Guest House of the University of Ghana, Legon, in Accra in 2011; and rewrote it once again at the Hoover Institution, Stanford University, in 2012. I wish to give special thanks to Eric Warner of the Russell Sage Foundation, E. Gyimah-Boadi of CDD, and David Brady of the Hoover Institution for supporting these efforts. My thanks go as well to the Weatherhead Center of Harvard University, which has repeatedly found the means to sustain this project. Marion Dumas and Eoin McGuirk read and commented on the manuscript. Deirdre McCloskey and Cormac O'Grada provided me with key bits of information on climate and grain markets. Thanks, too, to Richard Snyder of the Watson Institute at Brown University for organizing a conference around an earlier draft of the book. Feedback from Robert Blair and Janice Gallagher proved especially useful, enabling me to address key matters of logic, evidence, and interpretation. Thanks also to Alexander Noonan and Jennifer Backer, who helped to shepherd the manuscript from typescript to publication.

I wish to conclude by acknowledging my debt to four extraordinary scholars: Margaret Levi, Douglass North, Catherine Boone, and Charles Tilly. So powerfully have their insights influenced my thinking that I often mistake their ideas for my own.

The data collected when preparing this study can be downloaded from Harvard University's Dataverse. The address is dx.doi.org/10.7910/DVN/ZCPOOX.

1

Introduction

After pondering the disparity in income between rich nations and poor, Robert Lucas famously stated: "Once one starts to think about [the problem], it is difficult to think about anything else."[1] Humanitarians, policymakers, and scholars have joined Lucas in addressing the determinants of development; and in this volume, I, a political scientist, join them.

Among those who seek to account for the disparities in income that mark the modern world, economists, such as Lucas, stand supreme. Not only do they rank among the most skilled and insightful of those who study development, but also they dominate the agencies that fund programs and design policies for those who strive to achieve it. But clearly, the problems bedeviling efforts to promote prosperity in the developing world are not purely economic in nature. Some arise from cultural values and religious beliefs; others from biological and environmental forces; and still others from politics. I shall focus on the impact of politics. I shall focus in particular on politicians, their use of power, and their impact on development.

Development, I contend, contains two elements: one economic, the level of prosperity; and the second political, the degree of security. From this perspective, societies can be considered more developed the greater their prosperity and the more secure the lives and property of those who inhabit them. Some might object to the use of income, and especially average income, as a measure of development. But clearly the attainment of other valued outcomes is costly and prosperous societies are better positioned to secure them than are those that are poor. As for security, I take counsel from Hobbes, who noted that where "the life of man is nasty, poor, brutish and short," there is "no place for industries, because the future thereof is uncertain . . . no knowledge of the face of the earth; . . . no arts; no letters; and what is worst of all, continuous fear, and danger of violent death."[2] Both prosperity and security are valuable, then, not only in their own right but also because they make possible the attainment of other values.

Throughout this book, I probe the political foundations of development.

Method and Substance

Most who study development proceed "cross-sectionally"; that is, they compare poor nations to rich ones and note how differences in, say, education, gender equality, investment, or corruption relate to differences in standards of living. But development is a dynamic phenomenon and involves change over time. It is best studied, then, by seeing how nations evolve. Not only that: only a handful of nations in today's developing world have achieved a standard of living comparable to that of nations in the developed world; and in many, life and property remain imperiled. The number of "successes" is small; and because most of these reside in the Pacific Rim, so too is the amount of variation in the sample they provide. Today's world thus provides us little information. The implications are profound: today's world supplies little insight into how nations develop.

In response to this difficulty, I turn to history. Rather than proceeding cross-sectionally, and comparing poor countries with rich in the contemporary world, I proceed "longitudinally" and explore, for a given set of countries, how they changed over time. For reasons that I will soon discuss, I focus on England and France in the medieval and early modern periods. At the end of the latter, England stood poised to undergo the "great transformation" whereas France stood on the verge of political collapse. Attempts to isolate the factors that rendered the one more successful than the other can therefore offer insight into the factors that promote or impede the attainment of prosperity and security.

To use historical materials in this fashion, we have to assure ourselves that at least two conditions are met. The first is that the historical cases be sufficiently similar that inferences can be drawn from their divergent responses to similar stimuli. The second is to find a way of moving from "what is known"—the historical cases—to what cannot yet be known—the determinants of development in the contemporary world. We now turn to these issues.

TURNING TO HISTORY

The principal justification for drawing inferences from a comparison between England and France is that politically, economically, linguistically, and culturally, in the medieval and early modern periods, England and France shared important characteristics in common.

The England we first encounter was ruled by the Normans. And the Normans, like the Angevins that followed, presided

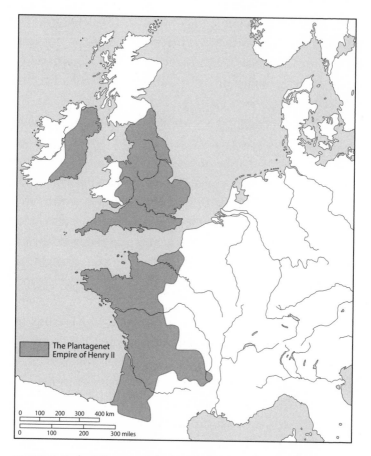

FIGURE 1.1. England, France, and the Angevin dynasty. *Source*: "Henry II, Plantagenet Empire" by Cartedaos (talk) 01:46, 14 September 2008 (UTC), own work. Licensed under CC BY-SA 3.0 via Wikimedia Commons.

not only over England but also over their "homelands" in what now is France (see figure 1.1). England's governing classes held properties on both sides of the channel, which they crossed and recrossed to manage and defend. The ruling lineages intermarried and incessantly fought each other. On both sides of the channel, the elite spoke the same language and until the sixteenth century belonged to the same church. That the two cases shared such basic characteristics in common, I argue, enables us to relate their differences to variations in the developmental outcomes that emerge over time: the one, becoming richer and more powerful; the other, a failed state.

USES OF THE PAST

Turning to a second challenge, we ask: How are we to employ our knowledge of history to gain insight into the contemporary world?

We do so by noting that in the medieval and early modern periods, Western societies were agrarian and that the underdeveloped nations remain largely so today. The attributes that commonly mark agrarian societies offer a framework that enables us to compare the two sets of cases; they enable us to treat them as members of a similar class. While accommodating, the framework (see box 1.1) is also powerful: it highlights regularities that enable us to draw on what is known about one set of cases to shed light on another. By so doing, it enables us to better comprehend the impact of power upon the process of development.

AGRARIAN ECONOMIES

As can be seen in box 1.1, two powerful regularities characterize agrarian economies, one governing production and the other consumption. The first is the law of diminishing returns. Derived by David Ricardo, a student of England's agrarian economy, the law states that as population grows, because the quantity of land remains fixed, per capita output declines. The first settlers would work the most productive land; as the

---

BOX 1.1. An Agrarian Society

The Economy. Rural economies abide by the law of diminishing returns. As populations grow, in the absence of technical change, incomes decline. And by Engel's law, poor people devote a greater percentage of their incomes to the consumption of food than do those who are better-off. Taken together, diminishing returns and Engel's law imply that if an economy is agrarian, its people will be poor.

The Society is organized by kinship.

> **Families** constitute the active agents of an agrarian society.
> **In the economy:** They control not only the spending but also the generation of income.
> **In the polity:** They govern the use of power.
> In addition, the nature of the assets they control shapes the preferences they hold.

From these characteristics, several phenomena emerge:

> **Migration:** To elude the impact of diminishing returns and thereby prosper, people migrate; they seek additional land. **Note the implication**: Contrary to common beliefs, agrarian societies are *not* static. People move frequently, either as families or hordes.
> **Specialization and Trade:** To elude the impact of diminishing returns, people specialize in production and exchange. They make intensive use of the productive factors with which they have been comparatively well endowed, be it meadows, wetlands, forests, or a position beside a waterway. Harvesting more than they wish to consume, they exchange the surplus for goods produced by others. **Note the implications**: (1) Not only farming but also trade takes place in agrarian societies. Not only farmers but also merchants inhabit them. In addition to farms, there are towns. (2) Relations between town and country mark the politics of agrarian societies. The two quarrel over the price of food: something that town dwellers buy and consume and that rural dwellers produce and sell.

---

population grows and people spread out, they then move to lands of lower quality. Should they instead remain on the most fertile plot, as their numbers increase, they would have to farm more intensively or make use of less productive labor, such as the aged. The increase in population therefore results in less output per unit of labor. By the law of diminishing returns, as this regularity is known, in agrarian societies, over time, average incomes decline and people become poor.[3]

The second law characterizes consumption. Named after Ernst Engel—a statistician who studied household economics in Germany—the law holds that the lower a person's income, the greater the percentage of her budget that she will spend on food. Food is a necessity, after all; to survive, a person must eat. Should she become poor, she will therefore curtail her expenditures on other commodities and devote her income to the purchase of food.[4]

The two laws pertain to individuals who produce and consume. While thus "micro" in scope, they generate "macrolevel" implications. By Engel's Law, poor societies are agrarian; and by the law of diminishing returns, agrarian societies become poor.[5] These regularities permeate both premodern Europe and the less developed portions of the contemporary world and mark them both as underdeveloped.

There are few laws in the social sciences. That two of the few we possess pertain to agrarian societies is fortuitous and encourages us to believe that premodern Europe and the contemporary developing world may abide by common logics. They encourage us to believe as well that insights extracted from the one can deepen our understanding of the other, even if the two inhabit different places and times.

From these laws, other regularities follow, and these too offer points of entry for those who wish to use history for the study of development. To fend off declines in income in agrarian societies, people specialize in production and engage in trade. One result is regional differentiation, with wine, say, being produced in one location; timber and charcoal in another; and meat, hides, and dairy products in yet a third. Another is commerce. As trade and markets span these diverse settings, they enable people to exchange the surpluses they produce locally for goods that may be produced more cheaply in other locations. In response to diminishing returns, people also migrate. They venture forth in search of new places to settle. As we shall see, regional differentiation and migration—both responses to decreasing returns—shaped the politics of development in medieval and early modern Europe and shapes it in the developing world today as well.

As suggested by Engel's Law, a third, "macrolevel" implication emerges: as incomes rise, the relative size of the rural sector declines. With development, agriculture gives way to industry and manufacturing, with factories replacing farms, towns displacing villages, and labor shifting from farming to commerce and industry. Development thus involves "structural change," in the words of some,[6] or a "great transformation," in the phrasing of others.[7] To study the political foundations of development is to study the politics of these changes.

Two economic "laws" thus provide a structure that enables us to place medieval and early modern Europe within the same framework as the contemporary developing world and to focus on a common set of themes: regional specialization, migration, and the impact of structural change.

A last major regularity characterizes agrarian societies. It is the importance of kinship. In both agrarian and industrial societies, families govern consumption; they allocate the household budget. But in agrarian societies, they govern production as well; they assign tasks in home and field to the members of the household. Kinship and the family also govern the polity. Offices and titles are transmitted by the rules of descent. Polities are often governed by dynasties and localities by groups of kin. And it is the family that provides security: by brandishing arms, its members deter those who might seek to encroach upon them.[8] When we study the economics and the politics of agrarian societies, be they in the historical West or the contemporary developing world, we shall focus on the role of the family.

Because of their agrarian nature, medieval and early modern Europe and the developing world share key features in common. This common set of features constitutes what I call a "political terrain": a setting within which politicians compete for power. As we shall see, the composition of that terrain determines what kinds of actions are "winning" and therefore how those with power are likely to behave. Examining the historical cases enables us to infer the features that appear to have led to the productive use of power in one case and to its destructive use in another, thus suggesting lessons that should inform our understanding of development in the contemporary world.

THE ROLE OF EMPIRE

Many will bridle at this approach. Conceding the presence of commonalities, they would also stress the importance of differences between medieval and early modern Europe and the developing world today. The challenge of development today differs from that in the past, they would contend, for nations today are attempting to develop in a world dominated by those who are far richer and more powerful than themselves.

By way of rejoinder, I advance two counterarguments. First, as does the developing world today, in the medieval and early modern periods, Europe confronted others whose wealth and power were greater than their own.[9] It felt threatened by the Caliphates, the Turks, and invaders from the steppes. It had lost holy shrines and religious capitals to those who fought in the name of a god other than their own. It was aware of the riches of "Cathay" and the Middle East and the power of those who invaded from the east and south. Europe thus emerged in a world dominated by societies wealthier and more powerful than itself. Second, I shall in fact stress the impact upon the developing world of its subjugation to Europe. And when doing so, I shall note how Europe's hegemony rendered the developing world similar to its "slow developing" predecessor—to France, that is, rather than to England.

Placing both the developing world and historical cases within a common frame thus enables us to levy insights from historical Europe, where development has been achieved, to the contemporary world, where for many development remains an aspiration.

We now move from matters of method to matters of substance.

Core Tension

Throughout this work, we note a pervasive tension—one that takes two forms. The first arises in societies in which power lies in private hands.

When security is provided by families, then development, we find, cannot be achieved. To achieve development, a society must be both prosperous and secure. But when private families control both production and coercion, then they must choose: to be secure, it is best that they possess little worth stealing. And should they wish to prosper, they had better prepare to fight, for others will seek to prey upon them.[10] In such societies, people can be prosperous or be secure. They find it difficult to be both.

As we shall see, this insight informs our understanding of institutional change. In medieval Europe, societies prospered, cities formed, farming became more profitable, and incomes rose.

But with the growth of prosperity came the spread of violence. The result was a demand for a new political order: the movement of the control of coercion from private hands to a central agency, capable of providing the peaceful settlements of disputes.

Once coercion is reorganized in this fashion, however, the tension between prosperity and political order rises in another form. For, as noted by Weingast, "a government strong enough to protect property rights is also strong enough to confiscate the wealth of its citizens."[11] For those who are interested in the political foundations of development, as am I, the central issue is thus how power is used and, in particular, whether it is employed to provide security and to underpin prosperity or to imperil and despoil. The comparison between England and France offers us insight into the factors that lead to different political choices and thus to different developmental outcomes. At the end of the early modern period, England was poised to enter an industrial revolution while France was poised for state failure.

The factors that appear to account for the difference in the manner in which power was employed in England and France cast light as well on the trajectories traced by Zambia and Kenya: the two cases we draw from the developing world. As is often the situation in the developing world, in these two countries, periods of rapid economic growth were followed by abrupt reversals. Given the attributes that Kenya and Zambia share with other agrarian polities and other portions of the postcolonial world, the factors that shaped the behavior of those who governed these two countries surely operate elsewhere, and in the last portion of the book I seek to isolate them.

Situating the Argument

The arguments I mount both echo and dissent from the works of others. Of greatest relevance is Huntington,[12] who, as do I, cautions that economic growth can be politically disruptive and lead to conflict between regions, between communities, and between town and country. Huntington too stresses the importance of political order and the need for institutions to achieve it. While my work therefore re-echoes his, I take a more historical turn. I strive, moreover, to explore the "microfoundations" of my arguments and how individual actions generate the collective outcomes we observe: poverty and disorder, on the one hand, and prosperity and security on the other. I am also far less sanguine than is he about the impact of hierarchical institutions and stress that while they may be necessary for achieving development, they clearly are not sufficient.

Acemoglu and Robinson, like Huntington, focus on the manner in which political institutions promote—or impede—economic development.[13] In advancing their arguments, they—as do I—turn to history. In contrast to Acemoglu and Robinson, however, I am less inclined to stress the impact of institutions and more inclined to stress the impact of other factors—economic and social—that shape political incentives and the use of power in agrarian societies. And I am also more inclined to draw upon agricultural economics and ethnography when doing so.

As do Acemoglu and Robinson, North, Wallis, and Weingast focus on the manner in which violence is used and organized.[14] And they, too, draw on materials from history to analyze contemporary development. In contrast to both Acemoglu and Robinson and me, North et al. make use of static typologies and view development as the process by which people move from "limited access" to an "open access" social orders. To a greater degree than they, however, I seek to base my explanations on the behavior of individuals, and in particular, on the behavior of those who possess political power. I seek to understand why in some settings political ambitions are better served by safeguarding life and property and promoting the creation of wealth, while in others, they are better served by using power to imperil or impoverish so that others might gain. By probing for "microfoundations," I seek to account for the impact of politics upon development.

Robert Brenner should also be counted among the economic historians who have influenced this work.[15] Where he sees class, however, I see power and, in particular, power in the forms it takes in agrarian societies: the power of families, of kin groups, and of regions. Those who aspire to rule in such societies must "win" politically; they must choose how best to act and to respond to the choices of others. And when they act, they influence the course of development. By reformulating Brenner's approach, I seek not only to compare cases within historical European history, as did he, but also to use those comparisons to clarify the political foundations of contemporary development.

In many ways, this study resonates with a last literature: that produced by the first generation of those who studied the politics of the developing world, such as Rupert Emerson, who addressed the breakup of empires; Anderson, Von der Mehden, Young, and Sklar, who focused on communalism and ethnicity; and Weiner, Rosberg, and Geertz, who wrote about political integration and the formation of states.[16] While these scholars perceptively captured the nature of the polities bequeathed by the breakup of empires, I hope that I have deepened our understanding of how their makeup shaped the behavior of those who, having captured power, then employed it and thereby shaped their development.

2

The Fundamental Tension

Viewed from afar, in the early medieval period, England and France traced similar developmental paths. Born of the Roman Empire, Britannia and Gaul, as they were then known, slowly recovered from the poverty that followed the Empire's collapse. As they did so, both faced a challenge that confronts all who aspire to develop: how to reconcile prosperity with security. Both responded by transforming their political institutions, shifting control over the means of coercion from the hands of families and placing it under the control of a central power.[1]

As I shall demonstrate in the chapter that follows, their paths then diverged. And because they initially exhibited important commonalities, when England and France begin to diverge, they then supply us with useful information. They then shed light on one of the perplexing problems of our time: Why do some nations develop while others fail to do so?

Agrarian Origins

Military force underpinned the Roman Empire. But positive inducements also played a role; and in the Empire's reaches, these inducements flowed, by and large, from the urban places that lay along the great waterways of Europe.

While some over whom Rome ruled conspired to overthrow their masters, others instead competed for preferment within these urban communities. By gaining prominence in a city, a man could become a citizen, thus entitling even a provincial to patronage from the center and access to the Empire's courts. Just as Islam would later provide a legal framework for trade throughout the Mediterranean, so in an earlier era did Roman law.[2]

By the third century, Rome's Western Empire had begun to disintegrate, however. Scientists note reductions in the concentration of heavy metals in samples drawn from ice sheets and swamplands, suggesting less mining and smelting. Marine archaeologists note fewer shipwrecks, suggesting a decline in trade.[3] Other scholars stress the impact of the plague, which hit with particular force in the towns.[4] The Western Empire was repeatedly threatened by invasion, as the Vandals, the Goths, and the Germans coursed from east to west, themselves menaced by marauders from the steppes and in search of new lands in which to settle.[5] Cut off by conflict from markets abroad, faced with a declining labor force, and increasingly burdened with taxes to fund its defense, the Western Empire weakened.

The nadir of the Empire marks the starting place for this study. As we plumb the subsequent rise of what were once Britannia and Gaul, we seek insights both into how the West recovered following the fall of Rome and into how, in the contemporary era, societies that are poor and insecure might also develop. In doing so, we shall explore the tensions between prosperity and security and the manner in which people seek to resolve them.

Pursuing Prosperity

Following the collapse of the Western Empire, the pursuit of prosperity took two forms: attempts to escape the law of diminishing returns and efforts to seize the goods of others. The first gave rise to a variety of economic activities, which we now address; the second led to political conflict, to which we subsequently turn.

By relocating their households on higher-quality lands or in lands less densely settled, people secured higher levels of per capita output. Some migrants trekked to the less populated east. Others responded to recruiters who sought to secure new tenants in their lands.[6] Still others drained wetlands or cleared forests. Opening new lands, settling new territories, and moving to less populated portions of the continent—rural producers from the intensively farmed core moved to the less densely settled periphery. They thereby sought to elude the impact of decreasing returns.

Europe's revival was also spurred by the adoption of new methods of farming. The invention of the collar and the use of plow horses; the introduction of the plowshare and the moldboard; the cultivation of more productive varieties—each resulted in greater yields. The revival of Europe's economy was thus marked not only by the expansion but also by the intensification of farming.[7]

Rural incomes also rose because of specialization and trade. Per capita output increased as each region specialized in producing goods in which it held a comparative advantage; when families produced more than needed for their own consumption, they then exchanged the surplus for goods made by others. Whittaker and Goody note that between the harvest and the preparation of the fields for the new season, residents of the Rouergue constructed and fired "elaborate kilns" and virtually "mass produce[d]" pottery.[8] Coleman notes the building of mills and forges, the blowing of glass, the fulling of wool, and the production of soap and salt by "farm" families.[9] Others add linen, beer, brick, paper, leather, and linseed oil to the list of goods produced by rural dwellers.[10] For the family, the result was greater income; for the economy, it was specialization and trade. Such "Smithian growth" provided yet another way of countering the impact of diminishing returns.[11]

The revival of Europe's economy was not only the product of the spirited efforts of those who dwelled within it, however; its growth was also the product of forces unleashed from without. In the Middle East, the dinar of the Abbasid Caliphate was honored along the routes running between the Mediterranean and Central Asia. With the consolidation of the Song dynasty in China, goods began to flow along what became known as the Silk Road, leading from East Asia to the Mediterranean and thence to Europe.[12] The city-states of Italy, particularly Venice, gained trading privileges in Byzantium, the Islamic world,[13] and the fairs were organized in northern France.[14] European merchants imported spices, silks, alum, and wax, exchanging them for hides, furs, timber, and, increasingly, linen and woolen cloth, much of it manufactured in Flanders. As we shall see, in Flanders and other portions of northern France, towns formed and prospered, rendering the region one of the most prosperous in the kingdom—and the site of frequent conflicts. In the period "between 1180 and 1220," Georges Duby writes, the economy of Europe achieved a "rate of progress" that has "never been equaled."[15]

We seek to use Europe's history—which is known—to inform our understanding of development today—which is unfolding still. Doing so, one of the lessons we learn is: "watch out!" For with the rise of prosperity in medieval Europe came the rise of widespread violence. In the next section, we explore its extent and nature.

Political Violence and Institutional Change

When the pursuit of wealth and security lie in private hands—that is, when both are the product of the family—we find that as prosperity grows, security declines. In this section, we learn that in order to achieve both, societies innovate: they remove the provision of security from the hands of private families and place it in the hands of a central authority. To secure prosperity and security, they forge the rudiments of the state.

FRANCE

In France, the growth of prosperity appears to have inspired the rural elite to concentrate their landholdings into estates, seeking thereby to transfer their property from one generation to the next.[16] To accomplish this, family heads sought to redefine the laws of descent and marriage: rights to property, they insisted, were to pass to the eldest surviving male and cousins were to be allowed—indeed, encouraged—to marry so that property rights would be retained within the stem family.

The concentration of ownership inevitably led to the loss of land rights among younger males. These changes led as well to an increasing number of unmarried youths with little stake in the social order. With few economic prospects but skilled in the martial arts, the young men began to maraud the countryside. Behaving as young warriors do, they bonded, drank, bragged, and raided; each band formed, if not a clan, then a fraternity. Trampling crops planted by farmers, driving merchants from the roads, and extorting produce and wine from the cellars of monasteries, they spread fear among those less able to fight.

In many instances, the resulting violence took on the character of the feud. Families recruited armed companies to defend their lands. They fed and boarded them and allowed them to wear their colors. The bands became brotherhoods. Imbued with the ethic of kinship, retaliation became an ethical imperative; wrongs *had* to be punished, not only to uphold the honor of the band but also to deter and thereby protect personal property. As the countryside grew more prosperous, it therefore became more violent.

In France, then, the period of rising prosperity was also the era of the chatelain: fortifications arose on every hillside and at every river bend, it seemed. The increase in violence reflected the increased value of land and the strength of the desire to seize or defend it.

THE PEACE

One response to the outbreak of violence was the demand for peace. Another was the attempt to forge an institution capable of using coercion to secure, rather than to imperil, life and property.

The demands for change took the form of "peace movements,"[17] many organized and sustained by the monastic orders. Monks and clergy numbered among the victims of the violence. Their monasteries were well worth looting and they were as defenseless as merchants and peasants. The church was in a position to respond: it was organized, it drew personnel from the upper ranks of society, and through its services it made regular and intimate contact with other portions of society. In reaction to the increasing violence, the clergy organized rallies, led marches, and issued pronouncements condemning private predation and exhorting the young warriors to redirect their efforts toward public service.[18] Prodded by the church, scholars resurrected the doctrine of the "just war," distinguishing between the private use of violence and its use for public purposes: the promotion of justice, the protection of the weak, and the defense of the vulnerable.[19] They thereby sought to transform thuggery into chivalry.[20]

While monks and clerics targeted the warriors and vassals, Abbot Suger of St. Denis took aim at the royal family. Through wise counsel, devoted service,[21] and persuasive preaching, Suger gained influence over the monarchs of his time. Not surprisingly, kings found attractive Suger's claims that their power was a gift from God. From this it followed that the means of coercion were therefore to be vested in their hands; power was to be centralized and rendered hierarchical; and force was to be used not for private advantage but rather in the service of social order.[22]

Economic as well as political considerations came into play. The royals found it useful to ally with the Church, the richest institution in Europe. In times of need, they could borrow its funds; in times of war, they could tax its wealth. Dispensing justice also proved remunerative: money that had been paid in compensation for damages could now be collected as fines. And given the values being championed by the clergy, the monarch now could justifiably turn against his own vassals; as the monarch now occupied an exalted rank, should his vassals challenge his authority, he now could legitimately punish them.

Rather than the means of violence remaining in private hands, then, the means of violence increasingly fell under the control of a central authority. Hierarchy joined kinship as a mode of political organization.

ENGLAND

In every era and in every place, it has been found, as household incomes begin to rise, so too does the demand for textiles. This was as true in medieval Europe as it was at the time of the industrial revolution. As Europe's population grew and its people enjoyed greater prosperity, the demand for wool also rose. Fibers from England were among the most prized; English wool found favor not only in Flanders, the center of Europe's expanding textile industry, but also in the Mediterranean and beyond. Given the increased profitability of wool production, monasteries and landed gentry expanded their holdings, and those who once had leased out land sought now asserted rights of ownership. The result was a flood of litigation and increases in conflict over land rights.

As shall be discussed in greater detail in the chapter that follows, compared to France, England was politically centralized. No Abbot Suger was necessary to flame the ambitions of William I or Henry II, and attempts to challenge their power were deemed—and treated—as treason. But in England, as elsewhere, succession to office took place through the family and it was therefore subject to the vagaries of biology. When Henry I died in 1135, he left no son. Two claimants stepped forward: his nephew Stephen, regarded as the leader of the Norman branch of the royal family; and Henry's daughter, Matilda, his sole surviving offspring, whom he had married into the Angevins, a lineage that ramified throughout much of southwestern France.

Both claimants had strong allies within England. Stephen enjoyed the backing of men who had served under Henry I, including those to whom he was closely related.[23] Matilda, for her part, enjoyed the support of Robert of Gloucester, her half brother, whose holdings extended over England's western border with Wales. In 1139 Matilda departed the continent to challenge Stephen's hold on England's throne. In the war that followed, Robert and his followers mobilized the southwest for Matilda.

The split within the royal family exacerbated tensions in the countryside, already riven with disputes over land. Once Stephen, as king, backed one party to such a dispute, Matilda, as challenger, could then gain backing from the other. The result was what historians call "The Anarchy"—a period in which private armies were formed, private castles were built, and fighting spread throughout the countryside.[24] In the words of the chronicler: "Every man built his castles" and "filled them with devils and evil men."[25]

When the Angevins captured the throne, the new monarch, Henry II, set out to pacify his possessions. He did so by enacting statutes designed to put an end to the feud. Should a family pursue private justice and seek revenge, it could be deemed to have committed a crime. Kin groups were still to play a major role, however; while no longer permitted to seek revenge, they were obligated to deliver their relatives to the king's courts, should they have become party to a dispute. Should the family fail to act as a bailiff, it then fell subject to the mercy of the king.

Under the new system of justice, violent acts were no longer private matters; they were no longer subject to private settlement. Rather, they constituted an offense against the political community, an entity that possessed a collective interest in peace, whose agent was the king.[26]

Conclusion

Engaging with materials from medieval Europe, we have been reminded of the degree to which families lie at the economic and political center of preindustrial societies. But we have also learned that while able to manage production and to perfect the arts of farming, the family was less able to provide security. The defense it provided came at a high cost. By threatening retaliation, it sought to check predation; but were its resolve to be tested, its acts of retaliation were likely to trigger a violent response, starting a costly feud.[27] The very manner in which it sought to provide security could instead generate additional conflict.

To prosper and be safe, our forebears appear to have understood, requires that private power give way to public power. In France, the Church argued that public welfare is best served by forgiving the offender—or by taking him to court. In England, assault became a crime against the state. In both, control over violence was vested in the center; and rather than remaining decentralized, violence was recast in hierarchical form.

In both France and England, then, we sense a phase change: a point in which development becomes possible. We see attempts to lay the political foundations for the preservation of security and prosperity.

Many, joining Tilly, locate the origins of the state in war.[28] But what we have learned here is that the origins of the Western state lie in the provision of "justice."[29]

In the last chapter, we noted features of agrarian societies. Thus far we have emphasized the central role of the family, both at the farm site and in the polity; the importance of migration and regional specialization; and the pervasive tension between prosperity and security. We have also noted the role of this tension in inspiring the transformation of power. Thus far, France and England appear to move in parallel, as it were. In the chapter that follows, we note that after the creation of hierarchy, the two countries then diverge. In the one, central power is used to safeguard and promote the creation of wealth; in the other, it is employed in a predatory manner. The reasons for this divergence will inform our understanding of development in the contemporary era.

3

Taming the Hierarchy?

In this chapter, we continue to examine preindustrial England and France in search of what the two cases can tell us about the political foundations of development. By the end of the early modern period, England was poised to enter the Great Transformation whereas France verged on state failure. In this chapter I argue that differences in the way those atop the central hierarchy made use of its power affected the course of their nation's development.

England

In the eighth century, Vikings settled in lands on the continent. But as their numbers grew, their fortunes declined. Not only did smaller holdings result in lower incomes (the result, of course, of diminishing returns); smaller holdings also resulted in smaller bequests. To counter their declining fortunes and to maintain control over restive offspring, family heads therefore migrated.[1]

In the case of the Vikings, migration often took the form of conquest. Word had reached them of the tens of thousands of livres raised by the English to keep the Danes at bay; clearly, England was prosperous. England's fighting forces, they learned, made use of outdated technology. The Normans—as the Vikings were known—had learned from the Franks how to use cavalry in battle, a skill not yet mastered by the Saxons of England. It was Edward the Confessor who provided the pretext and justification for their invasion. Ailing and increasingly incapacitated, he substituted political promises for military might and offered the right of succession to his throne to foreign leaders, if only they would refrain from invading. Among those leaders was William, Duke of Normandy. And when Edward died and Harold, the Saxon, claimed the throne, the Normans determined to unseat him.

While preparing for their invasion, the Normans worked to forge a more cohesive fighting force. To do so, the richest and most powerful among them redefined their ties of kinship. In pursuit of common interests, they created a legend of joint descent from one Gunor, a woman, and this in a society where descent had long been reckoned through males. Doing so led to the formation of a team sufficiently large to prevail in battle but sufficiently small that the booty seized need not be spread too thin. The myth served an additional purpose: it enabled the team to unite as a band of kin.[2]

By Searle's account, the Normans honed their skills by fighting in Blois, Anjou, and Flanders, dropping from their ranks the inept or fainthearted and settling upon William as their commander.[3] In 1066, they crossed the channel and invaded England. Defeating Harold and his army, they placed William on the throne.

When the Normans defeated the Anglo-Saxons, they defeated a polity that had itself conquered and subdued much of

England and created a means for administering its possessions. In the course of its expansion, the kingdom of Wessex had built an army and forged a revenue system capable of financing it. It had established armed townships to defend against invasion—burhs, as they were called—and carved out districts, known as shires, that were responsible for organizing the "hundreds"—settlements liable for taxation—and local governments, known as shire courts, to oversee local administration. Between the king and the localities stood *thegns,* knights who served in the king's administration during peace and commanded his forces during war. When the Normans invaded and defeated Harold and his army, they therefore seized a polity that was unified and well administered.[4]

After conquering England, the Normans rapidly thinned the ranks of its Anglo-Saxon hierarchy. So great was the purge that "English names fell from the rolls of the shires, to be replaced by the names of Normans."[5] To cow the remainder, the conquerors erected fortifications. William allocated these castles to his colleagues, along with sufficient land to maintain their battlements and to retain a company of soldiers. His team, it appears, remained small: when England's lands were apportioned, they divided them among the monarchy, the Church, and fewer than two hundred others.[6]

England was thus conquered by a cohesive group of venturers, engaged in migration and bound together by the prospects of material gain and putative ties of kinship. Whereas monarchs elsewhere might tower over their followers, in England, the king governed in concert with others. The barons were close allies and kin and as such possessed the right to speak and be heard. The political game in England was premised on hierarchy, then; but policy was not dictated. It was the product of deliberation among colleagues.

Because of its history of conquest—first by Wessex and then by Normandy—England had been rendered unified. The challenge was to occupy and consolidate the polity, not to assemble it. As shall be seen, the nature of this challenge affected the manner in which power was subsequently employed and how its use differed from that in France.

France

While in England the challenge facing the ruling family was to govern lands just conquered, in France the challenge confronting the House of Capet—the lineage that held the throne at the time—was that of recapturing territories that its predecessors had lost. Its monarchs sought to reassemble the lands that had once formed the largest province of Rome's Western Empire and the kingdom of the Carolingians, who comported themselves as Rome's successors.

DIVERSITY

The territory of France had been settled by people possessing different cultures—Norse, German, Goth, or Burgundian, for example. Each community possessed its own legend of migration and each spoke its own language—attributes, according to Max Weber, which characterize ethnic groups.[7] As late as the nineteenth century, the country remained linguistically diverse, with Catalan, Basque, and Provençal being spoken in the south; Breton and Norman in the west; and Bourguignon in the east, to note a few examples.[8] The regions differed religiously as well, something that led to brutal conflicts, as in the south in the thirteenth century and throughout much of the country in the sixteenth century.

No single family governed France. After Philip Augustus had cowed the castellans in Île-de-France, the Capets dominated the central portions of the kingdom. But in other regions, powerful families held sway: the House of Dreux in Brittany, the Tencavels in Languedoc, the Tallyrands in Perigord, the Martels in Anjou, and so on. Some descended from counts. Counts were officers of the crown, posted by the king to rule a portion of the kingdom. In France, a large portion of the counts became dukes: rulers of regions that they and their families held by right.

Not only were the regions culturally and politically distinctive; they were economically distinctive as well. Bordeaux specialized in the production of wine and traded with England, while southern France produced fabrics that were then exported to countries bordering the Mediterranean. But by far the most prosperous was Flanders. Flanders was the center of trade between Europe and the North Sea and Baltic, and its ports prospered not only from commerce but also from shipbuilding, warehousing, and the provision of financial services. Flanders was also the center of Europe's largest textile industry. Manufacturing took place not only in the cities but also in the countryside, as farmers turned to the production of clothing and household goods during lulls in the agricultural cycle.[9] Different portions of the country therefore acquired different economic interests and these interests covaried with cultural identities and familial ties.

INTEGRATION

The House of Capet founded their capital in Paris. They defeated and subdued the warlords who had built private defenses within Île-de-France; reaffirmed their title to revenues gleaned from its forests, tenancies, and tolls; and fortified the valleys traced by the Seine and the Loire—the routes most likely to be taken by political challengers. Seeking to extend their power from their own redoubt, they then invaded or intimidated the regions about them.

In addition to conquest, the royal family forged alliances that enabled it to weaken the hold of local rulers. The monarchs offered protection to monasteries, bishoprics, abbeys, and cathedrals: in the words of Baldwin, they thereby rendered them "advanced posts" from which they could extend their power within regions dominated by others.[10] The Capetians treated the towns in the same manner: they offered them immunity from local taxation and, for a price, conferred upon them the right to build fortifications, recruit militias, collect tolls and levy taxes, and try cases in their own courts.

When incorporating a territory, then, the Capetians often first threatened it militarily, then subverted it politically; once they had intimidated and undermined its rulers, they then negotiated. In contrast with the Normans, who had slaughtered the *thegns*, the French monarchs often left local families in power. In many instances, they acknowledged the right of the local courts—the parlements—to modify national laws in order to render them consistent with local law and custom.

When the Normans "migrated" to England, they seized it; they took it by conquest. When the House of Capet asserted its dominance over France, it conquered some portions while subverting and negotiating with others. It made use of kinship, exchanging brides with local leaders much as a chess player might exchange pawns. Rather than seizing France, the House of Capet assembled it.[11] The political terrain in France differed from that in England in that it was made up of distinctive regions.

DISCUSSION

Some might bridle at the contrast I draw. Scholars, after all, often write as if "the North" of England constituted a cohesive region. True: the north exhibited distinctive cultural attributes and occupied a distinctive political position, being charged with defending against the Scots. But politically it was divided and was riven by conflict. Underlying this conflict lay the rivalry between the Nevilles and the Percies, two of the most important families in the region and indeed in the realm. Both were rich and both were powerful; being marcher lords, they kept large numbers of men under arms. But their interests were national: they held lands not only in the north but also in the midlands (in the case of the Percies) and the west and south (in the case of the Nevilles).[12] And during the latter portions of the period addressed in this section, they backed rival branches of the royal family: the Percies, the Lancasters; the Nevilles, the Yorks.[13]

When the great families in England marshaled their forces, it was to exercise influence at the center. For the nobility, it was to gain a seat at the table; for a branch of the royal family, it was to occupy the chair at its head. In France, by contrast, when the great families marshaled their forces, their goal was to limit the writ of the center and so to nullify threats to the assets, customs, and laws of their region.

To appreciate the contrast, return to the case of Flanders. Its relative wealth made it a target for predatory families, such as the House of Burgundy. Upon the death of the Count of Flanders (1376), Philip the Bold became its duke.[14] From this base, the House of Burgundy exercised power at the highest level in France. When Charles VI descended into madness, Philip joined forces with the house of Orléans—the stem branch of the royal family—to administer the realm. The two families soon quarreled over issues of procedure and policy, however, and when their quarrel turned deadly, they, in the words of Duby, "tore the state apart."[15]

France and England thus exhibited contrasting political terrains, the one highly regional and the other not. As we shall see, because they thus differed, those atop their respective political hierarchies adopted different political strategies, thereby giving rise to different developmental outcomes. The best way to illustrate these differences is to examine the manner in which the monarchs intervened in their economies—something to which we now turn.

The Revenue Imperative

"Traditionally," monarchs paid for their wars using the revenues generated from their own lands: from the sale of wood and charcoal from their forests, for example, or from fees paid by tenants who had settled on their lands. They also raised revenues by licensing monopolies. In addition, at times of "necessity," kings could also seize goods, horses, livestock, and foodstuffs or levy "benevolences" from churches, villages, lords, and merchants, that is, loans they could repay at favorable rates and over long duration. In these ways, monarchs provisioned their military forces.

In the fourteenth century, however, intermittent combat gave way to campaigns and armies grew larger in size. The fixed costs of fighting rose. So too did the magnitude of shocks to the treasury, as when a monarch's forces suffered unexpected reversals or encountered opportunities too attractive to resist. To prevail in combat, monarchs could then no longer rely on the resources gleaned from their own lands or from intermittent levies; they needed to extract revenues from others and in greater amounts and to find new ways to borrow. They needed, in short, to create systems of public finance.

Throughout much of the medieval and early modern periods, England and France remained at war, and their governments were therefore in need of revenues. While their monarchs faced a similar challenge, they responded, as we shall see, in different ways. The manner in which they responded was shaped by the distinctive properties of the political settings within which they maneuvered. It was shaped by the political terrain.

ENGLAND

In England, the search for revenues led to a redefinition of the political "team," transforming its membership to include landowners and merchants from throughout the kingdom. At the center of this transformation lay the wool industry, which was reconfigured to serve as the tax base for financing the king's wars.

While the quality of wool produced in England varied by region, landowners turned to the rearing of sheep in virtually every portion of the nation. After the tumultuous reigns of Stephen and Matilda, commercial networks quickly reemerged, with the small-scale producers placing their wool with the large, who then consigned it to buyers from London. After accumulating sufficient stock, London's merchants then shipped the wool to the continent, where they sold it in markets in Bruges, Antwerp, or Ypres.

According to Power, one of the most discerning students of the wool industry, the political elite in England were "very early aware of their quasi-monopolistic position in the ... market." England, they recognized, was the largest producer of high-quality fiber. "A good part of the Italian cloth industry and almost the whole of the industry of the Low Lands," they realized, "depended on English wool."[16] Given England's standing in the market, were the kingdom to limit the export of wool, it could raise its price.[17] For the king, the implication was clear: were he to raise revenues by taxing wool, he would face less opposition than he would were he to tax other sources of income. For the tax would be shifted onto foreigners.

Controlling the wool market posed several challenges, however, and should they not be surmounted, the king's search for revenues would fail. Wool was shipped in bales, which, while bulky, could be moved and hidden. Those seeking to avoid the wool tax could therefore easily smuggle their produce abroad. How, then, was the market to be regulated? Clearly, the king and his agents needed to acquire an intimate knowledge of the wool industry and the cooperation of its members. They therefore organized meetings of those with vested interests in the industry.[18] By restricting the number of licenses and the quantity of exports authorized by each, they limited the export of wool, thereby increasing its price; and by selling these licenses, they raised revenues for the exchequer. The monarch also formed the "Company of the Staple" to control the wool trade; the revenues earned by this monopoly were to be transferred to his coffers.[19] At moments of particular need, moreover, using wool stocks as collateral, the king borrowed. In addition to enhancing the king's capacity to tax, the restructuring of the wool trade thus also enhanced his access to credit.[20]

As the monarch devised ways of securing revenues from the territories he ruled but did not own, three interests thus came into play: those of the king, the merchants, and the landowners. The three shared a common objective: military victory. They differed as to how to apportion the costs of its attainment. To address this issue, the king called for delegates from the shires to convene in London. Many consider this body England's first Parliament.

In conclusion, it is useful to note—and to stress—a major feature of the political institution forged to finance England's war: it helped further to align the great families—those who owned the land and dominated the countryside—with the central government. The heads of major families held seats in Parliament. And those that did not strongly influenced the selection of those who did.[21] Those who owned the land could thus shape the manner in which the monarch brought his power to bear on the income it generated and the manner, therefore, in which the state harnessed the economy to public purposes.[22]

FRANCE

The English thus forged a polity capable of eliciting the finances with which to fight and of binding rich and powerful families to the central political hierarchy. When the monarch in France intervened in his economy, however, he did so in ways that lowered its rate of growth. At the end of the early modern period, France was therefore less prosperous and less secure than was England.

When in 1356 the "Black Prince"—Edward of Woodstock—captured the French king, the dauphin (later to become Charles V) convened the Estates-General, an assembly whose consent was needed to impose taxes on territories falling outside of the king's demesne. The dauphin sought funds to pay the king's ransom and to return his army to the field, but the assembly fell into discord. It proved unable to agree on how to apportion the costs of defending the security of the realm.

Two principles governed the composition of the Estates-General. One was geographic: like the Parliament of England, the

Estates-General included representatives from each portion of the kingdom. The second was hierarchical: unlike Parliament, the Estates-General included representatives from the three estates: the clergy, the nobility, and the "third estate," consisting of merchants, lawyers, artisans, and the like. When Charles V convened a meeting of the body, conflict broke out between representatives from duchies in the west, which were militarily vulnerable and therefore willing to pay for military protection, and those from the center, and in particular Paris, which were relatively secure and so felt little need for it. Conflict also broke out between the estates, as each sought to shift the costs of war onto the others.[23] Adding to the challenge facing the monarch was the incompetence of the military. Given the army's record in the field, it was difficult for those deciding whether to contribute to believe that their sacrifice would provide a service of much value.

When later Charles VII faced an onslaught from the combined forces of England and the House of Burgundy, he too found himself in urgent need of funds. The war had shifted northward and now engulfed the central regions: Paris, now threatened, was therefore more inclined to support the king's requests. In recent campaigns, his army had won more battles; its record now encouraged those who might previously have been reluctant to back it financially. But the Estates-General remained configured as before and each estate again sought to shift the burden of paying for the war onto the others. To break the deadlock, Charles VII therefore revised his proposal: as originally planned, he would extend the *taille*—a land tax—to regions beyond his demesne; but, in doing so, he would exempt the aristocracy from paying it. The aristocracy thus achieved a victory: it shifted the burden of war finance onto others. And as the change was sufficient to obviate a veto by the Second Estate, the king secured much-needed revenues.

DISCUSSION

Seeking to finance their wars, the kings of England and France sought to extend their economic reach to encompass the greater polity. When they did so, they faced distinctive political terrains. In France, as compared to England, the terrain was marked by autonomous and powerful regional polities with interests of their own, some defined by the ambitions of their ruling families; others, by the nature of their economies; others by pride in their distinctive languages and cultures; and still others by an exceptional need for security, given their geographic location. Regional diversity made it difficult for the monarch to orchestrate collective agreements as to how to share the costs of national defense. Phrased differently, it made it difficult for the center to define and defend the national interest.

The economies of both nations were agrarian, and the monarchs' search for funds therefore brought them into conflict with the great landowning families. To finance its wars, the kings in England traded political influence for financial support. In France, they traded a privilege—exemption from taxes—for political quiescence. The political position of the landowners in France and England therefore differed. And as we shall now see, the two polities therefore began to trace divergent developmental trajectories.

The Great Transformation

Development begins with a "Great Transformation": the movement of resources from the rural to the urban sector as the farm gives way to the firm and the village to the city. The governments of both France and England faced competing demands from rural and urban interests, most obviously concerning the price of food. After describing and contrasting the policies they chose, we explore the political forces that shaped their choices. We then turn to the implications of those choices for their countries' development.

PROVISIONING THE CITY

In England, the collection, storage, and distribution of foodstuffs was governed by those who earned their incomes in the industry, be they farmers, butchers, millers, or transporters. This was true in much of France as well, with one major exception: in Paris, the government regulated markets, seeking thereby to assure the delivery to Paris of abundant and therefore low-priced food.

In France, the government built and maintained storage facilities in the districts about Paris and policed markets, bakeries, and warehouses in the city. As detailed by Kaplan, it insisted that private stocks be "visible," seeking thereby to prevent hoarding and rumors of shortages.[24] At times of dearth, however, government controls tightened. In response to Paris's needs, it banned the purchase of grain in the Paris basin by buyers from other parts of the country. It required that grain be stored in licensed warehouses and transported by licensed agents; and it insisted that once in the city, grain had to be sold in approved markets and baked in ovens registered by the government.

It was inevitable that once the government banned shipments out of the Paris region, shortages would appear in other markets. In response to outcries from Bordeaux, Nantes, and other urban centers, the government would again intervene, this time banning shipments abroad. It thereby diverted grain destined for export to local markets so as to assure ample supplies of food.

In England, by contrast, the government abstained from intervening in domestic markets. And when it did intervene, it did so by paying a bounty on exports, thus enabling the growers to sell profitably abroad even when prices overseas lay below those at home.[25] In France, the government favored urban consumers; in England, it favored the producers of foodstuffs.

The difference in policies reflects differences in the structures of power. In England, the agrarian elite was strongly vested in the government; by paying taxes, it had "purchased shares" that it then voted in Parliament. By contrast, the agrarian elite in France remained exempt from taxation; it had "cashed in its shares" and, in so doing, exited the political game. Rural producers were therefore well positioned to defend their interests at the national level in England but in a weak position to do so in France.

Important differences marked the "demand side" of the grain markets as well. While London and Paris were both capital cities, and therefore powerful, they were dominated by different interests. As noted by Brenner, in London, commercial interests dominated the government: "At least" thirty-two of the thirty-eight members of its Aldermanic Council—"an oligarchic body that essentially governed the city"—could be identified as merchants, he notes.[26] Paris, by contrast, was governed by its Parlement—a body dominated by lawyers and government employees.

In both capitals, members of the urban elite consumed but did not produce food. But while the merchants in England might spend a portion of their income on purchases of grain, many earned their income by trading in grain. And while the political elite in Paris aligned with other urban dwellers in demanding low-priced food, the political elite in London did not. Its members were more interested in the differentials between rather than in the levels of grain prices.

On the "supply side," the landed elite in England was powerful; in France, it was less so. And when the monarch in England adopted policies that benefited producers, he had little reason to fear the reaction of his capital, whereas the monarch in France was constrained from doing so by his fear of the reaction of Paris. In choosing their policies, then, the one adopted a "high price" policy and so favored the landed elite; the other exhibited "urban bias" and so favored policies that promised low-priced food.[27]

THE POLITICAL ORIGINS OF PROSPERITY

The "Great Transformation" refers to the change from an agrarian to an urban-industrial economy. What makes the transformation possible is technical change in agriculture. When productivity rises, farm families can release their young for jobs in the city. And if food is abundant and therefore inexpensive, disposable income can then rise, leading to an increased demand for manufactured products. An agrarian revolution thus lays the groundwork for the industrial revolution.

New Crops

In early modern Europe, the most significant innovations involved the introduction of new crops, particularly those that increased the quantity of nitrogen in the soils.[28] By introducing legumes, such as sainfoin, clover, or beans, farmers increased the fertility of their land.

Among the strongest incentives for introducing new methods is the prospect of increased profits. Prices therefore play a significant part in promoting technical change, and it is here that politics appears to have played a significant role. As we have seen, the government in England promoted grain exports and sheltered local markets from imports of low-priced grain. By contrast, in France, when grain prices rose, the government banned exports, thereby defending consumers against high prices for food. France adopted the "low price" policies that consumers preferred.

Given high food prices in England, the incentives to invest in new technologies were strong. The subsequent adoption of new farming practices led to increases in the supply of agricultural products; given that the demand for food is "price inelastic,"[29] the amount of food consumed remained relatively constant and prices therefore fell. In this way, the benefits of the innovations were shared with consumers.[30] As for France, evidence provided by Hoffman suggests that farms in the regions adjacent to Paris were as fully productive as the best farms in England. Farther from the capital, however—in the west and northwest, near Normandy and the lowlands, and in the northeast, near Belgium and Germany—the level of productivity remained low.[31] By the same logic as above, the relative stagnation of farming in France must have slowed the rise of disposable incomes in France's urban centers. It must have retarded the growth of France's urban economy.

Changes in Land Use

Many who championed technical progress in agriculture promoted not only the introduction of new crops but also new ways of managing the land. They advocated "mixed" farming, by which they meant rotating the use of land such that the grazing of livestock could be "folded into" the production of food crops.

The most ardent proponents of these new practices argued that the rotation between the production of livestock and food crops could best be achieved when fields were combined and farmlands enclosed. Securing a peaceful reallocation of land rights proved difficult to achieve, however, for it required that those who lost land be compensated in situations where adequate compensation was difficult to judge. Worse yet: even should a proposal appear equitable, participants had reason to hold out, hoping thereby to secure greater compensation for lands they were being asked to surrender. To secure the productivity gains on offer, those seeking to enclose therefore had to be able to impose settlements.

In England, given their control of Parliament, the large landowners were well positioned to mobilize the power of the state when seeking to alter the pattern of land use. They proposed legislation that enabled Members of Parliament to appoint commissioners whom they then empowered to draft plans for the reallocation of land in their districts. Once drawn up, the plans were then voted upon, with each person's vote being weighted by the size of his holdings. If over three-quarters of the votes were cast in favor of a plan, it was adopted. By weighting the votes by the size of landholdings, England's Parliament backed the effort of large farmers to enclose their lands.[32]

In France, by contrast, landowners were far less powerful. The case for enclosure was instead championed by public officials, particularly the intendants, officers appointed by the king to oversee the provinces and charged with—among other things—modernizing their economies.[33] When they found their initiatives stalled, the intendants then petitioned the courts. But their efforts were often in vain. Power in France had long been used to grant privileges and rights—rights to forests, pastureland, water, or transport—each of which had to be adjudicated in order to enclose. The process of enclosure was therefore arduous in France, and the intendants found the costs of legal fees exceeding the benefits from increased yields. The new technology therefore failed to spread in France as rapidly or as extensively as it did in England.[34]

Differences in the position of the landed elites and the power of consumers in England and France thus shaped the way in which their governments intervened in their economies. By affecting the rate and extent of innovation in agriculture, these policies affected as well the onset and pace of the Great Transformation.

Public Finance

Soon after Louis XIV invaded the Netherlands and the House of Orange replaced the Stuarts in England, France and England were once again at war. Although called by many the "second hundred years' war," their struggles could instead be called the first world war, for the conflict spread from the lowlands to central Europe and then to Asia and the Americas.

As had earlier been the case, the outbreak of war posed a fiscal as well as a military shock, and the two polities again reacted in different ways. The management of these wars served to further expose and to define the political structures that shaped their development.

TAXES

To fund his wars in France, the English monarch again turned to Parliament. Parliament imposed taxes on malt, beer, spirits, salt, candles, and leather. As portrayed by Brewer, these taxes were collected by trained professionals.[35] The monarch also secured a tax on land. While bargaining with Parliament, he offered in return measures designed to raise the price of grain.

He would, he pledged, regulate trade so as to ban imports of grain, should the foreign price lie below the domestic, and to permit its export, should it lie above.[36]

In France, too, the monarch sought to raise additional revenues. Having long refrained from convening the Estates-General, when he sought to raise taxes, he sought instead to secure assent from the regional assemblies. As recounted by Beik, the monarch opened these negotiations with an exorbitant demand; the regional assemblies would then counter with a lower offer, citing local conditions, such as drought, or longstanding privileges.[37] Often the result was a protracted standoff and a long delay in reaching agreement. The power of the regions not only made it difficult to agree upon a tax bill but it also made it difficult for the center to collect such taxes as were agreed upon. In many instances the regional assemblies rather than the king employed the tax collectors. Being local employees, they tended to underreport their collections and to inflate their costs, splitting their gains with the officials who employed them. The system employed to raise revenues for the king thus proved inefficient. It consumed time and effort, and revenues "evaporated" as they made their way to the fisc.[38]

As a result of faulty revenue collection, the French had to find other means of financing their wars. They, like the English, turned to borrowing.

PUBLIC DEBT

In England, Parliament created a bank with the power to finance the government's debt. The bank issued notes that could be freely traded in private markets. The relative ease and efficiency with which the government was able to collect taxes appears to have strengthened the public's confidence in the government's ability to meet its obligations, thus enabling the bank to access private savings inexpensively.

The French government also sought to borrow. The monarch sold the right to collect the salt tax to a group of financiers who, at his urging, formed a firm known as the *grandes gabelles*. He did the same with customs, selling the power to collect the tax to a group known as the *cinqs grosses firms*. The government then converted these companies into financial houses from which it could borrow on the surety of future tax collections. The king also borrowed from public institutions: towns, Estates (in the *pays d'état*), parlements, guilds, and the Church. In addition, he sold public offices, which also amounted to a loan: those purchasing the office exchanged present money for the fees that they would later collect by providing public services.[39]

In France, the monarch also reverted to default. After each war, he consolidated his debts. Each time he reorganized his finances, he chose the unit of account—that is, whether to value his obligations in gold or in silver—and selected whichever most reduced the amount that he had to repay.[40] He also added to the term of his loans, allowing himself to delay repayment. As stated by Bastable, "The history of loans [to the monarch can be] described as 'a history of bankruptcies.'"[41]

The process of default often took a theatrical turn: it was staged in court, with the government creditors being cast in the role of defendants. The government convened the Chambre de Justice, which rifled through ledgers and documents, enumerating the assets of those who held its debts. The Chambre sought evidence of corruption, and when it encountered reasons for suspicion, it struck, jailing those it accused and placing liens on their assets. Reduce or abandon your claims, it stated, or face ruin.[42]

In the face of such conduct, lenders demanded a "default premium," which resulted in lower prices for government

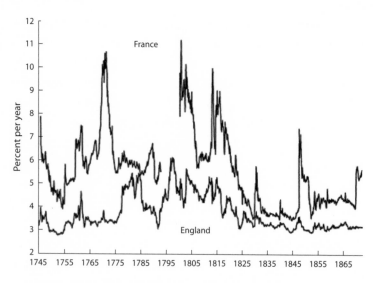

FIGURE 3.1. Monthly bond yields in France and England, 1746–1873.

securities and higher yields.[43] Given the political risk, the cost of capital remained relatively high and the returns relatively low by comparison with those incurred in England. Moreover, as much of the government's debt was held by public institutions, when it defaulted, it undermined its own base. As its debts mounted and default became more common, support for the government declined.

Conclusion

In this chapter, we have compared the development of France and England. At the outset, the economies of both were agrarian and therefore poor. But by the end of the eighteenth century, England was poised to enter the industrial revolution, whereas France was on the verge of state failure. Development, I have argued, requires prosperity and security, and England enjoyed more of both.

Seeking reasons for the divergent performance of the two nations, I have placed them within a common framework, one based on the attributes of agrarian societies. I stressed the impact of diminishing returns and of the response of people to it. In both the economy and the polity, I noted, key decisions were taken by families. Some responded by migrating: thus the peopling of France and the conquest of England. Others specialized in the production of goods in which they held a productive advantage: thus the creation of towns, wherein goods from one region could be exchanged for the produce from another. Other families specialized in the use of power: thus the creation of dynasties and the rise of local magnates.

While the two nations exhibited similar characteristics, these attributes manifested themselves in different ways, and those atop the political hierarchy therefore behaved differently as well. In England, the attributes of its agrarian society remained distinct; in France, they appeared in combination. In the latter, cultural differences overlay economic differences, and each region possessed its own political institutions. Regionalism therefore emerged as a force in France to a far greater degree than in England. The monarch in England therefore presided over a relatively homogeneous kingdom, while the monarch in France did not. The one could bargain collectively; in the face of regional opposition, the other did better seeking to intimidate on the one hand while conferring selective benefits—boons, privileges, or the like—on the other. Regionalism thus shaped the manner in which those atop the central hierarchy employed its power.

The politics of town and country also played out in different ways in the two countries. Because of the contrasting behavior of their agrarian elites and capital cities, the governments of England and France adopted different policies, with the result that technical change in agriculture proceeded more rapidly in England than in France. So too did the growth of urban prosperity.

In England and France, then, those atop the political hierarchy thus faced contrasting political terrains. Given the differences they faced, they used their power in different ways. While the king in England was able to assemble a coalition willing to invest in his ventures, the king of France, when he needed the wealth of the nation, had to seize it. Toward the end of the eighteenth century, England stood poised to enter the Great Transformation. France stood poised for state failure.

In the chapters that follow, I seek to employ the insights we have garnered from the comparison of these cases, drawn from the history of Europe, to analyze the challenges facing the developing world today.

4

Forging the Political Terrain

Before the mid-twentieth century, there was no "developing world."[1] Indicative is figure 4.1, which records the frequency with which the phrase "developing world" appeared over time in books scanned by Google.[2] While most of us regard the developing world as a fixed feature of global life, as suggested by the

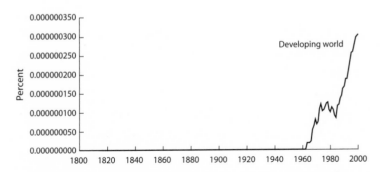

FIGURE 4.1. Ngram of references to the "developing world." "Percent" refers to the percent of two-word phrases that appear in books written in English and stored in libraries in the United States.

figure, in fact it is a recent creation.[3] It was forged by the West and emerged from its empires in the mid-twentieth century.

In this chapter, I discuss the origins of the developing world and the manner in which it was fashioned.

Rise and Collapse

Near the end of the fifteenth century, before he invaded Italy, Charles VIII first forged the archetype of a modern fighting force: an army built not around mercenaries and short-term recruits but rather professionals, grouped in units that combined foot soldiers with artillery, cavalry, and siege weapons and coordinated by an integrated chain of command. Provoked by his innovations, others soon emulated them and Europe's armed forces became both larger and more destructive. As their conflicts overran the boundaries of the continent, the nations of Europe began to probe the waters of Asia and the Americas, to acquire possessions there, and to fight in order to retain them.[4] To paraphrase the Marquess of Salisbury, most felt it better to quarrel abroad than to fight at home.[5]

First created in the early sixteenth century, Europe's overseas empires were thus born of political competition within the continent itself. By 1760, Europe had laid claim to one-twentieth of the world's population (figure 4.2); by 1830, it had seized one-fifth; and by the 1940s, it controlled more than one-third.[6]

A mere decade later, as a result of World War II, Europe's empires lay shattered. The Axis had been defeated, its territories occupied, and its cities destroyed. But the Allied nations too had been crippled by the war. Some, such as the Low Countries and much of France, had been fought over; and even those that had been spared militarily had suffered economically from having to bear the costs of the war. When after the war, their

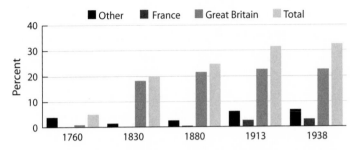

FIGURE 4.2. The spread of conquest. Percent global population ruled by imperial powers. *Source*: Calculated by the author, using data from A. Maddison, *The World Economy* (Paris: Organization for Economic Cooperation & Development, 2006).

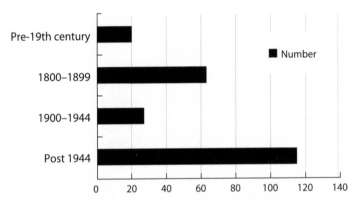

FIGURE 4.3. Birth of the developing world. Number of nations by date of independence as of 2000. *Source*: Calculated by the author, using data from D. Abernethy, *The Dynamics of Global Dominance: European Overseas Empires, 1415–1980* (New Haven: Yale University Press, 2000).

colonial subjects rose against them, the imperial powers were ill positioned to resist. And neither the USSR nor the United States—the two nations left standing, as it were—was willing to indulge the imperial pretensions of their former allies. By the late 1960s, over one hundred new countries therefore entered the global order, giving birth to the developing world (figure 4.3).

In this chapter, I describe how, having divided the globe, the European powers then governed it. The result, I argue, was the formation of polities that were culturally diverse and politically segmented and that exhibited high levels of regional inequality. In light of the preceding discussion of Europe in the premodern era, the implication is clear: the developing nations were configured by their colonial overlords in ways that led power to be employed following independence in ways that retarded their development.

The Imperial Origins of Diversity

In its typically breezy prose, *The Economist* once described how the European nations divided the Ottoman Empire. The boundaries of Iraq, Syria, Palestine, and Lebanon, it reminds us, "reflected not natural or human boundaries, but the whims and fears of the imperialists.... A northern slice, running from the Mediterranean to the Tigris river, went to France; a southern slice was bagged by the British . . . keen to put the French between them and the Russians to the north."[7] As anyone familiar with Africa well knows, the boundaries of its nations too were drawn by European diplomats gathered in Berlin, each seeking to slake his nation's thirst for prestige, wealth, and territory.[8]

Politically, the nations of Europe sought empires; economically, they were disinclined to spend much upon them. As noted by Brendon, the colonial office in England was often unable to compete for funds from the treasury: it "could at any time be overruled by the Admiralty, the War Office, the India Office, the Board of Trade, the Foreign Office, or the Treasury. The last of these often had the final word."[9] Instead, the occupiers often required the "natives" to pay the costs of being ruled by a foreign power. In West Africa, for example, Huillery finds, the local population was compelled to pay 98 percent of the costs of its own occupation.[10]

While little inclined to invest in territories once acquired, the colonial powers nonetheless appeared relentless in their quest to acquire more. In part, their insatiability was fueled by their need to preempt. The quest for empire represented, after all, an extension abroad of conflicts within Europe itself. What is more, from the vantage point of Europe, the rest of the world appeared like common—or at least unclaimed— territory, which strengthened each power's inclination to lay claim to a piece of land before another could do so.

Economic incentives also shaped the size of the territories to which the imperialists lay claim. While foreign occupation hardly qualifies as a "public service," foreign governments are subject to the same economic logic as are indigenous ones and also find that the average costs of governing decline the larger the number of persons they rule. Given their desire to govern at low cost, the European states therefore tended to gather the multitude of smaller, indigenous polities into larger entities.[11]

A combination of political and economic incentives thus resulted in the forging of a thin layer of foreign administration— and one often strapped for funds—atop a large and variegated political terrain. In South Asia, for example, the Dutch forged a single unit—Indonesia—from an archipelago of over 15,000 islands. In Africa, the Belgians merged over 200 tribes into a single polity called the Congo. And when the British drove in-land to subdue the Ashanti, they then created the Gold Coast: a tenth the size of the Congo but containing nearly 100 small polities and several indigenous states.

The most immediate concern of those on the ground was with political order. Not only was disorder costly to suppress and its damage costly to repair, but also it could attract the attention of others, eager to challenge for supremacy, given any sign of weakness. Adding to the threat of disorder was the composition of the imperial polities. Each community had previously been independent, its security the product of deterrence and the fear of reprisal. The imperial powers therefore needed ways to limit provocations that might trigger retaliation; they needed to introduce means of securing political restraint.

When doing so, the occupiers behaved as if guided by the arguments of James Fearon and David Laitin, who explore two systems for securing life and property: one based on deterrence and retaliation—the system in place at the time of the Europeans' arrival —and the other based on internal monitoring—the system favored by the occupiers.[12] The first system yields the feud; the second, self-policing. Under the first, retaliation follows harmful acts; but punishment can itself trigger reprisals, particularly when wrongly targeted. Violence may therefore spiral out of control. In the second, should a member of one group inflict harm upon someone in the other, then the offender's community is obliged to surrender the offender for punishment; as friends and relatives can distinguish between the innocent and the guilty more accurately than can strangers, their actions are less likely to provoke reprisals. Self-policing thereby reduces the threat of intergroup conflict. Rather than dismembering the polities they had conquered, the imperial regimes often preserved and empowered them instead.

The threat to peace came not only from conflict between indigenous communities but also from disputes within them. For this reason too, the imperialists found the local elite invaluable, for it was they who possessed the knowledge needed to keep the peace.

Consider, for example, the problem faced by a foreign administrator overseeing a local chieftaincy where political titles pass through the male line and in accord with seniority. The administrator would find the practice familiar, as it was also employed in much of Europe. But say that among the people he now ruled, men took multiple wives. And say that the firstborn male of a junior wife was born before the firstborn male of the senior wife. Which notion of seniority would then apply, that based on birth order or marriage? To resolve such issues, administrators often took counsel from locals; they knew that were they to fail to "get it right," they would plant the seed of future discord. By thus empowering locals to define "local law and custom," the colonial occupier traded power for peace and so reduced the costs of government.

In the Middle East, imperial governments ruled through khedives, beys, and pashas; in South Asia, through the Wadiyars, Nawabs, Nizams, and Inamdars. In Java, after conquering the Mataram Sultanate, the Dutch ruled through those who had once held positions within it. In Africa, they ruled through headmen and chiefs; and where they could find no rulers— that is, where there had been societies without states—they created them. They appointed chiefs among the Kikuyu and Ibo, for example, where few chiefs had previously ruled, and dispatched princes from southern kingdoms of Uganda to rule over the "acephalous" societies in the north. Only the British officially named this strategy, calling it "indirect rule," but it was followed in practice by virtually all the occupying powers.[13] In this manner, the European occupiers helped perpetuate subnational polities and empower elites at the local level.

The imperial powers also vested local elites with control over land. Ponder the teachings of C. K. Meek of the School of Oriental and African Studies (SOAS) in London. Historians, archaeologists, anthropologists, linguists, and "experienced hands" from the empire gathered at SOAS to share what they had learned with those preparing to enter the colonial service. Long stationed in Nigeria, Meek had closely observed the communities he governed and recorded what he had learned. Foremost among these lessons was the importance of leaving control over the land in the hands of those upon whom the government depended. As he states in *Land Law and Custom in the Colonies*: "The authority of chiefs, sub-chiefs and heads of clans and families is bound up with the land. . . . The control of land has as a consequence been one of the main planks of [British Rule]."[14]

While generally reluctant to spend on their overseas possessions, the imperial powers were willing to invest when large profits could be made by doing so. Mineral deposits in southern Africa; oil fields in the Middle East; or export crops—tea, coffee, or spices, for example—in Southeast Asia: productive regions benefited from the creation of roads and railways, ports, and public services. The result was the creation of a second form of regional diversity: not one based on cultural distinctions or political differences but rather on differences in income.

Regional diversity, subnational concentrations of power, elite families deeply vested in their communities, regional inequality: imperial rule forged in the colonies a political terrain that more closely resemble the political geography of France than that of England. Taking counsel from what we have learned from Europe when Europe too was agrarian and poor, the resemblance suggests that in the postimperial nations we should find power being used in ways that might impede their development.

Before we can seriously entertain this conjecture, we need to be more confident of our initial characterization. I therefore conclude this chapter by introducing numerical data. In the chapters that follow, I then turn to qualitative materials and probe two cases: Zambia and Kenya, two nations with which I am familiar.[15]

The Imperial Legacy

As is well known, by comparison with their former colonial masters, the developing nations are agrarian and poor. Figure 4.4 documents the phenomenon.

To document the additional features of the colonial legacy, I provide measures of ethnic composition, indirect rule, and regional inequality.[16] These data enable me to compare two sets of nations: those that had been colonies as of 1810[17] and those that had not. The first I refer to as "Colonial," "Post-Colonial," or "Post-Imperial." The latter set of nations I label as "Non-colonial," "European," or "Western."

As shown in figure 4.5, the postimperial nations not only are agrarian; they are culturally diverse. "Ethnic fractionalization"—column 1—is a measure of the likelihood that if two persons were selected at random from the population of a country, they would be members of different ethnic groups.[18] Column 2

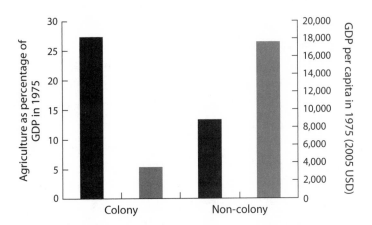

FIGURE 4.4. The agrarian nature of the postcolonial world. Average for colonies and non-colonies of agriculture as a percentage of GDP in 1975 and GDP per capita in 1975. *Source*: Data from http://data.worldbank.org/products/wdi.

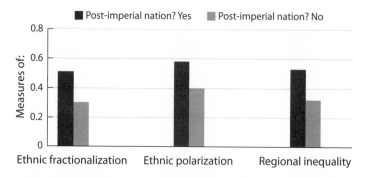

FIGURE 4.5. Imperial origins and regional diversity. Applying one-way analysis of variance to the data on ethnic fractionalization and polarization and standard tests of tabular distributions to the evidence of regional inequality indicate differences that are significant at the .01 level. *Sources*: Ethnic fractionalization: http://www .stanford.edu/~jfearon/. Ethnic polarization: J. G. Montalvo and M. Reynal-Querol, "Ethnic Polarization, Potential Conflict, and Civil Wars," *American Economic Review* 95, no. 3 (2005): 796–816. Regional inequality: from http://gecon .yale.edu.

reports data concerning an additional measure. As a nation's population gathers into two groups of equal size, the index grows larger. Studies have found that this measure bears a systematic and positive relationship with political conflict.[19] Lastly, column 3 introduces data regarding the presence or absence of regional inequality. To compile it, I drew on data compiled by William Nordhaus and his team at Yale University.[20] The data were gleaned from photographs taken during the night by satellites circulating the earth and then transformed into "light maps" (see figures 4.6–4.8 for examples). The intensity of illumination emanating from a region is suggested by the height of the peak projecting above it, and the height in turn suggests the level of economic activity within it.

Table 4.1 summarizes the numerical underpinnings for my argument. The level of ethnic fractionalization is rated as "high" when exceeding its mean (0.5). As can be seen from the table,

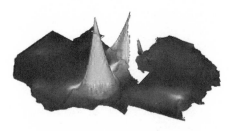

FIGURE 4.6. Regional inequality: Zambia. *Source*: http://gecon.yale.edu/sites /default/files/Zambia_3dmap.JPG?1273596309. Gecon project, William Nordhaus (Yale University) and Xi Chen (Quinnipaic University), project directors. Reprinted with permission from William Nordhaus.

FIGURE 4.7. Regional inequality: Ghana. *Source*: http://gecon.yale.edu/sites/default /files/Ghana_3dmap.JPG?1273592995. Gecon project, William Nordhaus (Yale University) and Xi Chen (Quinnipaic University), project directors. Reprinted with permission from William Nordhaus.

FIGURE 4.8. Regional Inequality: Argentina. *Source*: http://gecon.yale.edu/sites /default/files/Argentina_3dmap.JPG?1273605785. Gecon project, William Nordhaus (Yale University) and Xi Chen (Quinnipaic University), project directors. Reprinted with permission from William Nordhaus.

TABLE 4.1. The Imperial Legacy: Ethnic Fractionalization, Ethnic Polarization, and Regional Inequality by Colonial Status

	Ethnic Fractionalization		Ethnic Polarization		Regional Inequality	
	High[a]	Low	High[b]	Low	High	Low
Postcolonial[c]						
Yes	47	44	63	30	68	52
No	19	44	15	24	36	38
p-value[d]	0.009		0.003		0.302	

Note: The table lists the number of countries existent in 2012. The number of countries varies because of data limitations.

[a] Countries with high ethnic fractionalization scores are defined as those with ethnic fractionalization > 0.5.

[b] Countries with high ethnic polarization scores are defined as those with ethnic polarization > 0.5.

[c] Countries that were colonies at any point between 1800 and 2000, excluding Australia, Canada, and New Zealand.

[d] Significance levels calculated using the Fisher exact test.

among countries that once were colonies, by this measure, 52 percent exhibit high levels of ethnic diversity; among countries that avoided imperial rule, just 30 percent do so. Judging by the Fisher exact test, the difference is statistically significant. The level of ethnic polarization is judged high when its value exceeds 0.5. Among the postcolonial nations, 68 percent achieve this level; among countries that escaped colonization, only 39 percent do so. This difference too is statistically significant.[21] To answer the question "How concentrated is the regional distribution of income?" I empaneled a team of highly capable undergraduates. Using the "night lights" data, the team judged that more than half (57 percent) of the former colonies exhibited high levels of regional inequality, while among those who eluded Europe's imperial reach, slightly less than half (49 percent) did so. Although the difference is not statistically significant, the data indicate that postcolonial countries are more likely to exhibit high levels of regional inequality than are their former imperial masters.

Lastly, I also made use of data on indirect rule, shared with me by Jacob Hariri. "By indirect rule," Hariri writes, "I mean the incorporation of domestic institutions into the overall apparatus of colonial rule. Indirect rule features substantial delegation of authority from the colonial power to indigenous authorities."[22] Hariri's measure[23] is based on data taken from court cases and the ratio of court cases heard in traditional courts to the total number of cases. The measure exists for only thirty-three former British colonies. But because the form of colonial rule varied very systematically with the size of the European population, Hariri was able to construct a proxy for the degree of indirect rule in other colonies.[24] In the subsequent portions of this book, I make use of Hariri's data. But because they do not exist for the colonial powers or for nations that never were colonized, I do not include them in the table.

Conclusion

In this chapter, I have drawn on historical accounts and descriptive statistics to probe the nature of the political terrain that marks today's developing world. As had once been true of England and France, the developing nations are agrarian and (therefore) poor. They also bear features that were inscribed upon them by the colonial powers: high levels of cultural diversity, ethnic polarization, and regional inequality. I shall argue that within this political terrain, when politicians compete for positions atop the political hierarchy, they use power in ways that slow the growth of their citizens' income and render them insecure.

5

The Developing World

TWO EXAMPLES

In the chapters that follow, I turn to the developing world. In doing so, I draw materials from Zambia and Kenya, two countries in which I have conducted research. In this chapter, I explore their imperial origins and the political struggles that led to their independence. In the next, I explore their subsequent development. In both chapters, I assume a local vantage point and focus on the behavior of families in two communities: the Luapula Valley in Zambia and Kiambu district in Kenya. Tracing their responses to the opportunities before them, I note how they apportioned their energies between the pursuit of prosperity and the exercise of power, thereby helping to liberate their nations and shaping their development.

Born of Europe

ZAMBIA

Like other developing countries, Zambia[1] was born from conflict among the nations of Europe. Because of the rapid rise of

Germany in the nineteenth century, political tensions rose on the continent and led to competition for territories abroad. Given the rivalries between France and England on the one hand and their conflict with Germany on the other, the European powers looked for ways to reduce the prospects for war. Africa was one of the regions in which their ambitions clashed, and in Belgium, they found a useful arbitrator. The territories in Africa to which Belgium laid claim, they noted, could serve as a buffer between their own. They therefore conceded to Leopold, Belgium's king, much of the Congo basin—a region over which they might otherwise have come to blows.[2]

Zambia's history, like that of other territories in southern Africa, was shaped by Leopold on the one hand and by Cecil John Rhodes on the other. Rhodes learned of the legendary wealth of an area called Katanga, which lay in the southern portion of Congo (figure 5.1), and had sent a team to treat with one Msiri, then the most powerful chief in the region. To Rhodes's chagrin, he found that Leopold's agents had arrived before his own; rather than forcibly contesting each other's claims, Rhodes and Leopold agreed to share holdings in corporations that might later work the deposits. While the deposits in Katanga soon proved valuable, those in Northern Rhodesia initially did not and Rhodes therefore ceded them to the British government. Rhodes's corporations retained mineral rights, however, and when subsequent exploration uncovered evidence of rich deposits of copper, they invested in their development. The result was the creation of the Copperbelt (see figure 5.1), as the region became known; along with Katanga, it became one of the richest mining regions in the globe.[3]

When the British assumed control of Northern Rhodesia, they encountered a high plateau crossed by rivers, dotted with swamplands and lakes, and populated by recent arrivals. Some,

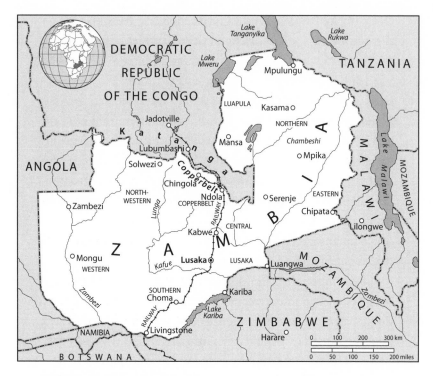

FIGURE 5.1. Zambia and Congo. *Source*: http://www.nationsonline.org/oneworld /map/zambia-administrative-map.htm.

like the Ngoni in the east, were fugitives of the Mfecane, the great nineteenth-century wars in southern Africa; others, like the Balovale in the west, were participants in the Angolan slave trade; and others, such as the Lunda, had migrated from Katanga, thereby extending the reach of the Lunda kingdom from the Congo to Northern Rhodesia. When we turn our attention to the local level, it is on the Lunda that we shall concentrate.

At the end of the Great Depression another flow of migrants then entered Zambia: whites, or "Europeans," as they were known, many coming to work in the mines and others to farm along the line-of-rail that linked Northern Rhodesia with South Africa.

These migrations seeded Zambia's political terrain with diverse communities, each with its own language, culture, and legends of departure and arrival, and some with their own ruling families.[4]

KENYA

Rivalries within Europe also gave rise to Kenya. In the late nineteenth century, Egypt and the Suez Canal provided a focal point for these conflicts.[5] Egypt depended for its water upon the Nile, and to secure military control over its headwaters the British constructed a railway from Mombasa to the interior, enabling them, should the need arise, to move troops from India to Uganda (see figure 5.2). Working with the British Cotton Growing Association, the government encouraged the planting, ginning, and export of cotton in the interior. In addition, it recruited settlers to establish farms along the rail line. After World War I, it settled former officers in the territory, seeking thereby to promote agricultural production and generate enough rail traffic to cover the costs of the railway.[6]

The city of Nairobi became the center of wealth and power in Kenya. It contained the administration and repair shops for the railways and the headquarters of the government's principal departments. The businesses that supplied the settlers' farms were also located there, as were the firms that purchased and processed their produce. Nairobi was where the settlers came to settle their accounts, to stock up on supplies, and to socialize. As the colony developed, the city grew. It came to occupy a

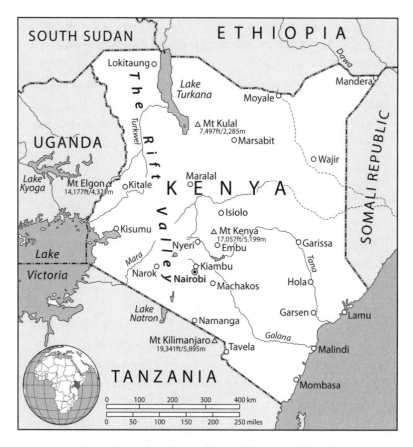

FIGURE 5.2. Kenya. *Source*: http://www.glpinc.org/Classroom%20Activities
/Kenya%20Articles/kenya-map.jpeg.jpg.

position in Kenya comparable to that of the Copperbelt in Zambia; it came to drive the colony's economy—and its politics.

Like Zambia, Kenya was populated by immigrants. Some
were Bantu speaking and entered Kenya, it is thought, from the
southwest. Of greatest interest to us are the Kikuyu, who settled
in the foothills and on the slopes of Mt. Kenya (figure 5.2).[7] Others spoke Nilotic languages and entered from the northwest.
Most relevant here are those now known as the Kalenjin, who

migrated to Kenya from the central Nile. While initially traveling in small groups, the migrants banded into larger ones, some becoming known as the Pokot, others as the Nandi, and so on. In response to threats from others—first the Maasai, then the white settlers, and then the Kikuyu—these groups coalesced into a yet larger, single group, called the Kalenjin.[8] As we shall see, the Kikuyu and the Kalenjin were both to play a major role in the postindependence period.

Regional Inequality

In both Zambia and Kenya, imperialism shaped the regional distribution of income. As in other developing areas, it rendered the distribution unequal. By focusing on the Copperbelt in Zambia and Nairobi in Kenya, we seek to gain insight into the impact of that inequality. As we shall learn, it was powerful. It was transmitted through the family and led to yet further migration, the reshaping of the family, and conflict.

To comprehend the impact of these "privileged regions," we focus on two rural communities: one, Luapula (figure 5.1), resides in Zambia and lies distant from the Copperbelt; the other, Kiambu (figure 5.2), resides in Kenya and abuts Nairobi.

ZAMBIA

In the period discussed herein, the Copperbelt consisted of five cities: Ndola, Kitwe, Chingola, Luanshya, and Mufulira.[9] Each town, save Ndola, contained a copper mine, and Ndola was the site of a large refinery. As already suggested, there is good reason to include Katanga and its mining towns in this discussion of the Copperbelt. The two shared a border and their mines lay but a short distance apart. The boards of the mining companies in Zambia included representatives from the Union-Minière du Haut Congo (Union-Minière or UMHK for short), a company formed to extract and refine the ores of Katanga.[10] The UMHK shared ownership of a railway linking the mines on the Copperbelt to ports on the Atlantic, while the mines in Northern Rhodesia had joined with the UMHK to invest in hydroelectric plants, thus assuring themselves of a supply of electricity.

In addition to the economic links between Katanga and Northern Rhodesia, there were political ties. One set ran through the indigenous communities. The paramount chief of the Lunda, Mwata Yamvo, resided in Katanga, but as a result of the Lunda migration, one of the most powerful of his chiefs, Mwata Kazembe, resided in the Luapula Province in Zambia. Other ties ran through the white settler communities who dominated politics in the two regions and opposed the rise of African nationalism in both territories.

Luapula

On the periphery of this mineralized region lie the rural areas of Zambia. Among them is the Luapula Valley, on which we will focus.

The recorded history of the region dates to the eighteenth century when Mwata Kazembe, a senior chief in the Lunda Empire, established his capital there. Mwata forged alliances with the powerful Bemba on the adjacent plateau, and they dispatched warriors to assist him in defending the valley from slave traders. As a result of Mwata's ability to withstand the slavers, people flocked to his kingdom in search of refuge.[11] Centuries later, more people arrived. For with access to the river and lakes—Mweru in the north and Bangweulu in the south—those living in the valley were well positioned to market fish to the residents of the mining towns.

While some residents of the valley fish, virtually all farm. The local demand for marketed food is limited, however, and the cost of transport to the mining towns high, making it unprofitable to export agricultural produce. As the population of the valley increased, families in the valley therefore fell victim to the law of diminishing returns. As have others throughout history, many therefore left Luapula and went in search of work in the mines. The export of labor underpins the valley's economy. It also shapes the structure of its families and the nature of their politics.

The Family and Migration

In Luapula, families expect that when their offspring mature they will migrate to the towns. During childhood, the migrant is prepared by family and kin to compete in the urban labor market. In effect, the family provides a way of investing in the young and forming human capital.

Figure 5.3 captures in schematic form a flow of resources within the family and over time. Focusing on the first generation (T_0), we see that the middle-aged transfer resources to the young. When the young then become middle-aged (at T_1), they in turn support those who had previously raised them, while also raising a new generation. Transfers between generations then continue (T_3 on) as the family reproduces itself over time.

In Luapula, the members of the working-age generation not only feed and clothe the young; they also invest in them. They do so by paying for their education. Following several years of schooling, the family possesses an educated child with the skills necessary to compete for a job in town—and to repay with interest the funds initially expended.[12] The repayment takes the form of remittances that flow from migrants in town back to the valley, thus helping to support the elderly.

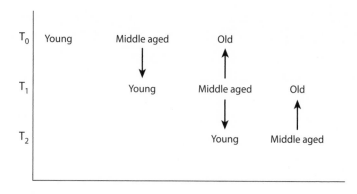

FIGURE 5.3. Overlapping generations and capital formation.

In this manner, families living in the village become a means for investing in the urban labor market. Data collected from Kasumpa village in the valley suggested than an "additional year's schooling . . . results in an additional K8 per annum in remittance. Assuming a work life of 26 years (age 20 to 45) and a discount rate of 0.05, the return to this additional year would be valued at K120; if the earnings are discounted at 0.08 per year, the returns are then in the neighborhood of K90."[13]

The lands that are now Zambia, we have shown, were once hit by an exogenous shock: the intrusion of foreign capital. Families in the valley responded by augmenting bonds of kinship with financial ties, thereby transforming themselves into a means for investing. As I shall now argue, additional factors then came into play, and these added a political dimension to the role of the family.

Land, Family Heads, and Power

As we have seen, for political reasons, colonial governments tended to favor "collective" as opposed to private ownership of land. In Zambia and other mineral states, the government had economic reasons as well to favor collective rights in property: it sought to shift the costs of social insurance to those it ruled.

The economics of mining is highly cyclical; it is linked to fluctuations in the business cycle. In times of prosperity, the demand for metal rises and mines hire additional labor. In times of recession, demand slumps, output declines, and the mines lay off workers. The government depended on the mines for its revenues, and when workers were dismissed, it bore the costs of supporting them. As a result, when economic conditions declined, the government faced the prospect of increased expenditures just as its revenues declined.

In Zambia, as in other mineral states, the government found a way of eluding this dilemma: it empowered urban dwellers to claim land rights, based on their membership in an ethnic community. If laid off by the mining companies, workers then could simply return to the rural communities from which they came. By vesting control over the land in "traditional authorities," the colonial governments therefore not only enhanced their ability to govern the rural population but also relieved themselves of the need to provide social insurance to those who lived in town.

When I worked in Luapula, I found people well aware of the "boom and bust" nature of the mining industry. They were also aware of the physical dangers of working there and that a rock fall, a splash of acid, a break in a steam pipe, or a mugging on payday could result in a disabling injury. Urban employment may be remunerative, Luapula's sons and daughters realized, but it was also risky. Migrants to the town therefore sought to secure rights to land in the valley: the ability to move back to the countryside constituted their safety net. The young as well as those of working age thus had a stake in the land.

Recall the "model" of the family (figure 5.3): transfers to the younger generation take place at T_0 and T_1 in expectation of returns at T_1 and T_2, respectively. In the first period, the young will of course promise to repay; what needs to be explained is why the middle-aged would believe them. For the family to insure the incomes of those intending to work in the city, its members must have some way of discerning when such promises are credible. And it was by mediating their access to land that the seniors gained the power to enforce the contract between generations.

One way of making such promises credible is to make the future prospects of the young depend upon actions by their elders. In Luapula, when a member of the younger generation retires and returns to the village in search of land, his fate then depends upon the elders' answer to the question: Can members of the family confirm that supplicant is *kumwesu*, that is, "one of ours"?[14] For the answer to be yes, the returning migrant has to be a member in good standing of a local family. He has to be legitimate, which means that his parents had been properly married, with sufficient degrees of separation between bride and groom and with bride wealth fully paid. In addition, he had to have been initiated into the community, either by undergoing traditional rites or by being baptized and confirmed. Those who control access to the land would also want to know: Had the migrant stayed in touch while living "abroad"? Had he sent letters, money, photographs, gifts? Had he come back to the village for funerals or weddings? Had he taken in young relatives while they attended school in town or offered room and board to others from the village while they searched for jobs? Was the migrant "one of us"? Was he a member of the community?

When planning their futures, the young could thus anticipate that the community and their family would at some point be asked to testify on their behalf. Because "family membership" was vetted and required testimony by seniors, those who invested in the future of the young could be confident that the young would repay. The family therefore provided a way of contracting for insurance, relieving the government of the burden of bearing the risks associated with mining.

At any point in time, families, and especially their oldest members, therefore provided the underpinnings of the labor market and the formation of capital. By doing so, they helped define the interests of those who lived in the valley.

KIAMBU, KENYA

Turning to Kenya, we focus on another community: Kiambu, a district that virtually borders Nairobi. Proximity to the city enabled the residents of Kiambu to do what those in Luapula could not: sell produce to those in town. Some residents sold charcoal; others vegetables, fruits, or maize; and those living in higher elevations supplied wattle to those wishing to mend the roofs or walls of their houses in the townships.[15] A fortunate few accumulated enough to purchase lorries and, with funds raised from transporting goods and people to town, to open stores and start businesses in the townships. As noted by Cowen, a commercially minded rural "bourgeois" therefore began to emerge from the ranks of the Kiambu community. Among the Kikuyu, Kiambu became known for the wealth of its businessmen.[16]

While some thus prospered from proximity to Nairobi, others did not. Hardest hurt were those who, with the arrival of the British, lost their land. Shortly before British arrived, a plague had struck cattle in East Africa and pastoralists seeking to restock their herds began raiding the cattle of others. Seeking safety, the Kikuyu moved to higher elevations. Seeing the lands at the lower elevations unoccupied and believing them unowned, the British had seized them. And lacking formal records, indigenous families could not document which lands were unoccupied and which were unowned.

Over time, the population of Kiambu grew and its lands became crowded. In keeping with the law of diminishing returns, the average income of its families declined. The "reserves"—the areas in which Africans could claim land rights—became notorious for their poverty. While Kiambu gave rise to a wealthy few, it became home to numerous poor.[17]

One response was migration. A second was the restructuring of the family. As we shall see, both responses shaped the colony's politics. And both constituted a prelude to violence.

Migration

The Kikuyu owned livestock and, compared to food crops, livestock make more extensive use of the land.[18] In an effort to prevent damaging people's crops, those in charge of the family's herds therefore moved them away from the villages. Over time, many moved with their herds to the Rift Valley.

When the Europeans settled in the Rift, they seized large acreages. Much of the valley was therefore sparsely settled, and the settlers initially welcomed those who moved in from the reserves. Not only did the herders provide much-needed labor, but also their livestock, while grazing, prevented the bush from reclaiming the grasslands.[19]

The Transformation of the Family

Over time, however, the settlers became less welcoming. Emulating their predecessors in early modern Europe, the European farmers began to integrate livestock into arable production. Prodded by the agriculturalists at Egerton College, they increasingly turned to "mixed farming" and produced dairy products as well as grain and food crops. They then profited not only from milk sales to Nairobi but also from higher yields of grain, given the increased fertility of the land once planted with fodder crops.

While beneficial for the settlers, the introduction of mixed farming proved disastrous for their Kikuyu workers. Their livestock were native to the region and were therefore resistant to local diseases. But the settlers' livestock were "exotics"; they were the offspring of cattle bred largely in Europe. Should an insect feast on the blood of an indigenous animal and then on the blood of one introduced to the region, the latter was likely to sicken or die. The herders, the settlers decided, were therefore to be cleared from the farms on which they had settled. They were to be sent back to the districts from which they had emigrated, including Kiambu.

Recall, however, that in Kiambu, their "homeland" had become densely populated. On the one hand, much of the land about Nairobi had been seized by settlers; in addition, the indigenous population had grown. There therefore remained little land on which to settle the refugees from the valley. In addition, landownership had become more concentrated. In the words of Cowen,[20] a "rural bourgeoisie" had accumulated large holdings. Many had benefited from European education. Known as the *athomi*, they knew English and could read—an advantage that offered great benefits when processing licenses, interpreting regulations, vetting contracts, and drafting titles to land. Serving as intermediaries between the colonial administration and the locals, headmen, and chiefs, the literates used their positions to accumulate wealth, power—and land.

When the herders returned to Kiambu, they therefore found themselves unwelcome. Rights to land were vested in families, and many of the families were unwilling to subdivide their holdings to accommodate now-distant relatives. The returnees, they argued, were better classified as *ahoi*—that is, tenants— rather than as family members and therefore had no claim to a share of the family estate.

Zambia and Kenya thus bore one of the characteristic marks of imperialism: regional inequality. As in other agrarian societies, the result was migration. As illustrated by our cases, while families organized the process of migration, they were also transformed by it. In Luapula, the solidarity of the family was enhanced; in Kiambu, families were fractured. As we shall see, in both regions, the transformation of the family constituted a prelude to violence.

The Politicization of Agrarian Societies

We have emphasized the way in which the structure of the family facilitates an escape from diminishing returns. We now argue that in pursuit of their economic interests, families enter politics. To advance this claim, we return to Luapula and Kiambu. In the case of Kiambu, we focus on an elite family, one that led the struggle for independence and then assumed high office. When we return to Luapula, we focus on the families of the "common folk" and note the role they played in the struggle for Zambia's independence.

KIAMBU

In Kenya, as elsewhere in the empire, the British adopted the policy of "indirect rule." No matter that the ethnic groups in Kenya lacked chiefs. The more conveniently to govern, the British created the post and filled it with graduates from schools run by missionaries.

In Kiambu, the government appointed as chief one Koinange wa Mbiyu. An astute and ambitious *athomi*, he was devoted to the promotion of Christian values and Western education. Koinange possessed a private agenda as well: the return of his family's lands, seized by the Europeans after it had retreated from the lower plains to escape the disease and warfare that marked the late nineteenth century. Initially, Koinange believed his British masters just; but when they repeatedly rebuffed his pleas, he became embittered.

After resigning from the colonial service, Koinange turned to business and politics. Taking advantage of Kiambu's location adjacent Nairobi, he supplied wood for building houses, charcoal for heating homes, and produce for consumption by those who living in town. He also organized a concerted campaign to recover the lands taken from his family by European settlers. The better to advance his claims in court, he invested in the talents of one Kamau wa Ngengi, an ambitious and gifted young man and a student of the history of the Kikuyu. Later to be known as Jomo Kenyatta, Kamau proved a capable witness at trials over land disputes and a dedicated lieutenant in Koinange's struggles to defend and extend his own holdings.[21]

Repeatedly rebuffed in their efforts to recover their land, the Koinange family switched from litigation to political action. The family became the spokesman for the interests of the region and its people. On the one hand, they launched a political party, the Kenya African Union (KAU). On the other, they continued to invest in the career of Jomo Kenyatta. They paid for him to study in England, where Kenyatta came to know members of the Pan-African Movement—George Padmore, Léopold Senghor, and Nnamdi Azikiwe, among others—and published a study of the Kikuyu.[22] Upon returning to Kenya, Kenyatta assumed the presidency of the KAU while also marrying Koinange's daughter.

The Koinange family had become a political force. It possessed both a political party and a formidable advocate.

To lend impetus to their campaign against the settlers, the Koinanges allied with the landless: the squatters who had been driven off the land by settlers in the Rift and the *ahoi* in Kiambu. They, the "haves," opened their political movement to the "have-nots" and championed their cause.[23] The result was an eruption of violence—part insurgency, part civil war—that became known as Mau Mau.

Mau Mau was but one of the many uprisings that marked the downfall of the British Empire. Along with uprisings in Palestine, Malaysia, and Aden, it helped deplete the national treasury and led England to abandon its territories abroad. While it therefore played a role in Kenya similar to that played out by other rebel movements, Mau Mau was shaped by forces that operated within a specific agrarian society—the Kikuyu—and in a particular place—the Central Province of Kenya. It was regional in nature.

To win their battle against white settlers and recover their rights to land, the Koinanges forged an alliance between an elite family—themselves—and the landless. As we shall see in the chapter that follows, in the postindependence period, Kenyatta was to pursue a similar strategy. But by the postindependence period, the white settlers were a spent force; it was the Kalenjin who dominated the Rift. The conflict that then threatened was not a war of national liberation; it was civil war.

LUAPULA

In Kenya, the liberation movement focused on the white settlers and their appropriation of land. In Zambia, the liberation movement focused on the white settlers and their control of the wealth of the mines.[24]

In the early 1950s, England created the Federation of Rhodesia and Nyasaland, joining Northern Rhodesia, Southern Rhodesia, and Nyasaland into a single polity. Taking advantage of electoral rules that virtually disenfranchised the African majorities in the three colonies, the European settlers dominated both the regional and federal governments and used their power to extract revenues from the Copperbelt and to channel them into public services for the whites. The liberation movement in Northern Rhodesia therefore sought the breakup of the Federation. Given their numbers, the Africans could control Northern Rhodesia, its leaders realized, and gain control over the revenues generated by the mines.

While agreeing on the goal of independence, those who led the liberation movement were nonetheless divided. One branch, known as the African National Congress (ANC), was "moderate." It included white politicians in the ranks of its leadership and strove to assure the Europeans—many of whom had invested in businesses and farms—of its commitment to property rights. In this period of global confrontation between communism and capitalism, the ANC received funding from the West. The other branch consisted of "militants," who gathered into the United National Independence Party (UNIP). With funding from the East and the support of the non-aligned states, UNIP advocated government intervention in the economy and showed less concern with safeguarding property rights. ANC's base lay in the more prosperous regions in Zambia: the Central and Southern provinces on the line-of-rail and portions of the Copperbelt.[25] The poorer provinces, such as Luapula, lay off the line-of-rail and backed UNIP, the party of the militants.

In the Luapula Valley, the goal of the liberation struggle was to assure the residents of access to the revenues of the mines. As we shall see, in pursuit of this goal, the liberation movement had to counter opposition from four sources: Katanga, the European settler community, the mine workers' union, and the traditional elite. No single region, especially one so poor and distant from the core of the country, could deal with such a combination of forces and the local leaders in Luapula therefore allied with a national party. The party they backed was UNIP.

We now turn to each of these threats. We then note how the residents' responses transformed the valley into a center of militant support for the nationalist movement.

Katanga

When Katanga withdrew from the Congo, the Belgians, who had ruled it, retained a strong presence in the province. Through the UMHK, they retained control over the mines.[26] In addition, they formed an alliance with Moise Tshombe, a prominent African politician. Tshombe was a member of the royal family of the Lunda; son-in-law of Mwata Yamvo, paramount chief of the tribe; and head of CONAKAT (Confederation des Associations Tribales du Katanga), a political party that dominated Katangan politics and championed the interests of his tribe.

In the election held prior to independence in the Congo, Tshombe and his party gained the majority of seats in Katanga's provincial assembly. Both Tshombe and the mining companies feared that if the Congo were endowed with a strong central government, politicians from poorer regions would use its power to prey upon the wealth of their region. When the Congo became independent, Tshombe, for political reasons, and the UMHK, for economic, therefore sought to render it a federal state. After their proposals for a decentralized government were rejected,

Tshombe declared Katanga independent. He soon began to meddle in the politics of Northern Rhodesia and to cultivate relationships with the Rhodesias' settler communities.

The Settlers

In Northern Rhodesia, African politicians determined to break the settlers' hold on the mines, and toward that end determined to take Northern Rhodesia out of the Federation. The leaders of the settler community responded by advocating the creation of a new federation: one that, in their words, would be wealthy enough to maintain "civilized standards" of governance and service provision in the midst of Africa. They proposed that Katanga and the Copperbelt join with an independent Southern Rhodesia and gave their political backing to those politicians, black or white, who would aid them in attaining this objective.[27]

The residents of Luapula feared that should the Copperbelt join Katanga in a new federation, they would lose access to the wealth of the mines. No doubt they would still be employed; but they, as foreigners, would possesses fewer rights and the revenues generated by the mines would be channeled to the white minority.[28] For reasons of pride and self-interest, they therefore sought to dismantle the existing Federation and to block the formation of a new one. By breaking free of federal institutions, they could divest the settlers of their control of the mines.

Mine Workers' Union

A third threat came from the mine workers' union and specifically from Lawrence Katilungu, its able and ambitious leader. The union was widely regarded as the most powerful labor organization in Central Africa. With branches at each mine, it played a major role in the region's richest industry. While thus possessing power, under Katilungu's leadership, the union deployed it with caution. Katilungu was willing to call for a strike if it would yield higher wages and improved working conditions, and he had repeatedly demonstrated his skill in organizing work stoppages. But he preferred—and was known to prefer—to bargain; he judged strikes to be costly and, if not aimed at "bread and butter" issues, wasteful. He was reluctant to call his men out over political issues, and many in management had come to respect his leadership and to view him as an asset.[29]

As Britain began to withdraw from Central Africa, local political forces started to coalesce about the president of the mine workers' union, encouraging him to enter politics. Industrialists and foreign intelligence services provided him funding, some of which they channeled through Moise Tshombe.[30] As noted above, Tshombe's political base lay among the Lunda and when Katilungu began to build an organization of his own, he too turned to that tribe. He repeatedly ventured into the Luapula Valley to pay his respects to Mwata Kazembe, the most powerful Lunda chief in the country.

Mwata Kazembe

Faithful to their policy of indirect rule, when the British occupied Northern Rhodesia, they ruled the people of Luapula through their paramount chief, and Mwata Kazembe served his people well. He protected and developed the fisheries; granted land to the missionaries, who opened schools; and championed the maintenance of roads and public health measures. The British served Mwata's interests in return. Not only did they pay him and back him when he was confronted by unruly subjects, they also allowed him to appoint Lunda aristocrats to govern the villages of "foreigners" who had settled in the valley, placing the immigrant communities directly under his rule.[31] Mwata thereby consolidated his hold on the valley and gained access to greater revenues.[32]

During the liberation struggle, attitudes toward Mwata Kazembe were shaped not only by his deference to the colonial overlords and the way in which he governed but also by his ties with Katanga. People noted the exchange of delegations and gifts between Mwata Kazembe's palace in Luapula and Mwata Yamvo's in Katanga.[33]

Thus did forces emerge and combine and so drag Luapula into the vortex of the liberation struggle.

The Response

Those in the valley who sought to secure the mines and to achieve an independent Zambia therefore faced a variety of threats. There was no way that the residents of the valley could counter them on their own. Instead they allied with a national party, UNIP, which was able to mobilize forces to oppose the machinations originating from Katanga. The locals, for their part, dealt with the power of Mwata Kazembe. And the two combined to counter the threat posed by the president of the mine workers' union.

Contra Katanga. UNIP found a variety of patrons abroad. It attracted support and funding from Egypt, India, and other non-aligned countries; and with the arrival of "Eastern-bloc" forces in the Congo, it gained the support of socialist governments as well. It thereby added its voice to that of others who urged the United Nations to intervene against Tshombe, thereby helping to neutralizing the threat he posed to Zambia's mines and thus to those, such as the residents of the valley, who depended upon them.

Contra Mwata. To undermine Mwata's rule, UNIP targeted the "stranger" communities in the valley, many of whom were descended from the soldiers who had been recruited to defend against those seeking to capture slaves. After settling in the valley, these communities were ruled by the descendants of the chiefs who had first led them. As already noted, however, Mwata Kazembe set those chiefs aside and appointed members of his court to govern the immigrant communities—an action that deeply angered those who disliked being ruled by "foreigners." When UNIP set out to organize the valley, it therefore concentrated its efforts on these communities.

UNIP targeted the fisheries as well. Prodded by the Department of Game and Fisheries, Mwata Kazembe had imposed limits on the seine size of nets, banned the use of poisons, and restricted the issuance of licenses. The fishermen deeply opposed these measures and often quarreled with the fish guards who imposed them. The fishermen too turned against their Lunda overlords.

Mwata Kazembe constituted a link in a chain that tied the Lunda in Zambia with their homeland in Katanga. By undermining his power, UNIP weakened the bonds that linked Tshombe's mineral state with the Rhodesias.

Contra the Mine Workers' Union. As for Katilungu, the liberation movement had taken his measure and found ample reason to fear him. UNIP therefore worked with Katilungu's opponents in the mine workers' union and those who, for a variety of reasons, might wish to unseat him. At the urging of UNIP, the Roan Antelope branch of the mine workers' union voted to dismiss him from office.[34] Other branches then joined in censoring Katilungu, and he was driven from the union's presidency.

Katilungu's political ambitions remained undiminished, however, and in November 1961 he started out from the Copperbelt on a trip to the valley, his vehicle loaded with "gifts" for Mwata Kazembe. He never arrived: he was killed when his vehicle was struck head-on. According to my sources, the vehicle that hit his was driven by local members of UNIP's youth league, dispatched, it was said, by their leaders to kill him.[35]

Toward Violence. Each initiative provoked a response by the government, which in turn exacerbated the residents of the valley. The police became political targets. Easily identifiable and often reviled, they were set upon as they moved along the trails, patrolled fish camps, or bicycled along the roads that stretched along the valley. Orchestrating their campaigns with those launched in other parts of the country, local activists unleashed wave after wave of violence. They harassed and abused those who failed to take part in protest marches and political demonstrations. They burned bridges, felled trees across roads, and destroyed schools throughout the valley. Having heard of Mau Mau, they imitated its insurgents, dressing in skins and stylizing their hair to resemble its forest fighters.[36] The government responded by flying in troops from neighboring Rhodesia. Its forces moved from village to village; in each, they employed local confederates to identify the political organizers, whom they then jailed.

Little did the government suspect, however, that the women of the valley were as militant as the men. It therefore left them in place while detaining their fathers, brothers, and sons. Nor did they recognize the significance of the structure of the families. In Luapula, descent was matrilineal: property and office descended through the female line. And marriage was patrilocal: a bride moved to the village of her husband. As a result, the interests of a family ramified from one village to the next in the valley. By the rules that defined its structure, the family therefore facilitated action at the regional level. Even given the arrest of a village's male leadership, the capacity for collective action in the valley remained intact.

In both Kenya and Zambia, the parties that drove the British from these portions of their empire did so through violence. In Kenya, Mau Mau took up arms. In Zambia, the liberation movement promoted civil disobedience in the urban areas and physical violence in the rural, thereby rendering the country ungovernable. In both places, the British retreated. In the early 1960s, both Zambia and Kenya departed the British Empire and joined the global community.

Conclusion

In both Kenya and Zambia, the political terrain was shaped by migration, a force generated locally, and by imperialism, a force originating from without. The former populated the land with culturally diverse peoples; the second rendered them unequal. Within the setting thus populated and endowed, families struggled to enhance their prospects, both economic and political. The result, as we have seen, was migration, violence, and the creation of two nations. Two decades after the end of World War II, Zambia and Kenya joined the developing world. In the chapter that follows, I analyze how politics then shaped their performance.

6

The Use of Power

Kenya and Zambia achieved independence in the early 1960s. Those who had led the political struggle then confronted the question: What use would they make of the power they now commanded? To answer this question, I focus on the behavior of Kenneth Kaunda of Zambia and Jomo Kenyatta of Kenya, who served as their nations' first presidents. I characterize the policies they pursued, seek to account for the choices they made, and note the impact of their decisions on their countries' development.

At the time of independence, both polities contained regions whose people differed in terms of their cultural heritages and resource endowments. To prevail politically, then, both Kenyatta and Kaunda had to reach beyond their own constituencies and gain support from other portions of the polity. Because of the high level of cultural and economic diversity, both confronted limits on their ability to do so and challenges, therefore, to their efforts to remain atop the political hierarchy. This chapter focuses on the way in which they responded to the challenges they faced and on the impact of their choices upon their nations' development.

Core Constituencies

Upon independence, Kenyatta's constituency was Kiambu, the district in Central Province in which he was born; Kaunda's was the United National Independence Party (UNIP),[1] which he had helped build and led to power upon achieving independence.

KENYA

As noted in the previous chapter, Kiambu bordered Nairobi, the largest city in Kenya and indeed in East Africa. Kenyatta thus came from a prosperous region. His constituency was split economically and politically, however. It included rich "bourgeois" who owned farms, firms, and commercial properties, many of whom had "sat out" the freedom struggle. To Kenyatta's discomfort, his constituency also included former freedom fighters, who remained poor and landless. While the freedom fighters lacked material resources, they commanded a moral authority that made them powerful. Lastly, his constituency included peasant farmers who had benefited from the imperialists' efforts to pacify the region. To temper local opposition to their rule, the British had promoted small-farmer agriculture.[2] They had surveyed and demarcated household plots, issued titles to the land, and trained and hired agricultural agents to promote the production of cash crops. The roads they had built to facilitate the deployment of troops also served the needs of local farmers. As a result, in Central Province, an energetic population of small farmers had emerged from the refuse of war.

As Kenyatta labored to consolidate his political base, he committed his government to programs that targeted each group. Following independence, he helped his wealthy compatriots acquire the estates abandoned by white settlers. Destined to become known as "telephone farmers," the new owners often worked in Nairobi, leaving their farms to be run by managers, recruited by the banks that held their mortgages. Under his presidency, agencies that had once supported white settlers began to support the production of cash crops by small, African farmers as well; families began to set aside portions of their farms to produce coffee, others to produce tea, and still others dairy products.[3] Kenyatta also backed the formation of settlement schemes, designed to benefit the former freedom fighters. Some were formal and run by the government; others were informal and sponsored by members of his province's elite.[4] Virtually all were located in the Rift Valley, which, being more lightly populated than Central Province, had long served as the destination for those seeking to escape the latter's confines.

By channeling valuable resources to each of these groups, Kenyatta lay the foundations for his political dominance in Central Province. The politics of the province remained unsettled, however, as political tensions persisted. Some were of long standing and permeated relationships between the three groups. Others emerged as a by-product of Kenyatta's attempts to extend his base from his home province to other regions in Kenya. At the center of both lay the former freedom fighters.

Many of the smallholders in Central Province feared and despised the freedom fighters; the liberation struggle had been as much a civil war as it had been a war for independence. Many of the wealthy viewed the former freedom fighters as competitors for the "fruits of independence." Both knew that having rebelled against their imperial overlords, the freedom fighters felt entitled to the lands that had been abandoned by those they had defeated. Both also worried that the former Mau Mau warriors might invade their farms or steal their livestock.

It was in part to relieve such tensions that Kenyatta encouraged his prosperous colleagues to invest in the resettlement schemes. Insofar as the landless could be resettled in other regions of Kenya, he appears to have calculated, tensions within his core constituency should decline. But insofar as he sought to promote emigration, Kenyatta intensified tensions between his core constituency and the Rift Valley, thereby making it more difficult to extend his political reach to other portions of his country.

ZAMBIA

Kaunda served as general secretary and president of UNIP. His constituency was not a particular region; it was UNIP's Central Committee. True, he had grown up in Chinsali, a town in Northern Province, and he spoke Chi-Bemba as if it were his native tongue. But his parents had migrated to Zambia from Malawi to take positions in a local school, and he spoke their language, Chi-Nyanja, as well. Rather than a locale, Kaunda's constituency was an organization: a liberation movement-cum-political party that he had built and managed.[5]

UNIP had broken away from the African National Congress (ANC), a party that drew its support from areas along the line-of-rail (see figure 5.1). Given their access to low-cost transport and their proximity to urban markets, those living in that region prospered from growing crops for sale in the Copperbelt and Lusaka. UNIP drew its support from provinces that lay beyond the line-of-rail. These provinces lay sufficiently far from the central regions that they could not profitably supply them with agricultural products and were poor as a result.

As general secretary and then president of UNIP, Kaunda presided over its Central Committee. Most members of the Central Committee came from districts off the line-of-rail. The electoral base of the party and the composition of its Central Committee was thus such that Kaunda did best by catering to the interests of the poorer regions of Zambia.

When Kaunda sought to gain support nationally, he, as had Kenyatta, then faced a political dilemma. Kenyatta became caught between Central Province and the Rift. Kaunda became caught between the poorer regions off the line-of-rail and the Copperbelt. To remain in power, both presidents needed the support of regions beyond their core constituency. Driven by the contradictions they faced, they—as we shall see—devised policies that they hoped would enable them to win politically. And when those policies failed, they altered the rules of the political game.

Political Instruments

When seeking to build a political base, Kenyatta and Kaunda made use of powerful political instruments. In this section, I describe these instruments and in the next examine how the two leaders employed them.

KENYA

When Kenyatta became president, he assumed control over what, for the developing world, was a sophisticated administrative structure.

Historically, the government in Kenya had catered to the demands of an affluent and vocal settler community. It had therefore created ministries of agriculture, transport, finance, justice, local government, labor, education, health, lands, and so on. In addition, the colonial government had fought—and defeated—a major insurgency; even large portions of the rural areas were therefore subject to "intensive administration."

At the lowest levels of this administration stood the districts. Above them came the provinces, where provincial commissioners ruled as if proconsuls.[6] They reported directly to the president and served as his eyes, his ears, and his chief enforcers. Responsible for political security, they could permit or prohibit public meetings; regulate the distribution of grain; control the movement of people or goods by road or rail; and dispatch the police and security services, be it to hunt down rustlers, pursue bandits, apprehend smugglers, or quell demonstrations.

Kenyatta's government had inherited the tools forged by the colonial regime. As Cold War rivalries spread from Europe to postindependence African states, foreign advisors helped Kenya's government form bureaus capable of monitoring Kenyatta's foes and their relationships with foreign governments—and of eliminating those posing a threat to his regime.

ZAMBIA

As in Kenya, politics in central Africa had been dominated by white settlers. Most had resided in Southern Rhodesia, however, and the number of settlers in Northern Rhodesia remained relatively small; so too, then, did the size of the latter's administration. When Kaunda became president, he therefore took charge of a far less elaborate administrative apparatus than did Kenyatta.

If only for this reason, when Kaunda sought to build a political base, he turned to his party rather than to the government. UNIP built and maintained an organization that extended from its headquarters in Lusaka to the townships in the cities and to villages in the countryside.[7]

I once conducted research in Kitwe, a mining town in the Copperbelt. There were three electoral constituencies in Kitwe and each contained three to five party branches; each branch was broken down into several sections; each section contained several "ten-house" units.[8] Three hierarchies spanned these several levels: a Women's Brigade, a Youth Brigade, and the Main Body, the last of which was run by the married men. At each level, each of these hierarchies was overseen by a party official who had been dispatched to Kitwe from the party's headquarters in the capital.

In the urban areas, the job of the party was to provide security, which meant monitoring expatriates, whose loyalty to the new government remained suspect, and Africans who might support a rival political party. It also meant quieting drunks and apprehending troublemakers. Most commonly, it meant keeping peace, especially in the markets, where crowds gathered daily, thieves circulated, and people paid close attention to the weighing and pricing of goods. The cost of living, and especially the price of food, numbered among the most sensitive issues in the townships.

When I shifted my field site from the Copperbelt to Luapula, I found the region far less densely settled than the urban townships and the party organization correspondingly less complex.[9] Rather than containing a network of sections, branches, and regional units, in a village, the party might contain but a single branch. Here the "hue and cry" sufficed for keeping order: there were no public markets, and as villagers produced much of what they consumed, they were less likely to protest high prices. In the villages, the party therefore undertook fewer tasks that affected day-to-day life than it did in town.[10]

As one of the founders of UNIP and general secretary of the party, Kaunda had helped build this apparatus. The party and its Central Committee constituted his core constituency. It also served as his key political instrument. It provided him the means to disseminate his policies, to monitor and cow those who might oppose them, and to entice or enforce obedience to his wishes.

Catering to the Core

When the two leaders employed the political instruments at their command, they implemented policies that catered to the opportunities and responded to the constraints offered to them by the political terrain.

KENYA

Kenyatta continued to back his prosperous colleagues. Recall that following independence, his government helped politicians and businessmen from Central Province to purchase the farms of the departing settlers. Having done so, most joined the Kenya National Farmers Union (KNFU), which served as an intermediary between the government and the commercial farmers. In 1975, the government had left the prices unchanged, and the KNFU resolved to lobby for a large price increase in the following year. Rather than approaching the bureaucrats in the Ministry of Agriculture, the union's representatives approached Kenyatta directly. After a "cordial meeting," the union was accorded a 20 percent increase in the price of wheat and an increase of 23 percent in the price of maize. Kenyatta thus rewarded the "telephone farmers"—the elite component of his core constituency.[11]

In addition, Kenyatta continued to champion a "small farm" strategy. For the coffee farmers, he charged the Coffee Board with marketing their crop[12] and securing better yields and fewer losses from disease or infestation. He promoted the formation of cooperatives, making them responsible for transporting and processing the harvest and distributing the proceeds from its sale at auction. Those who produced tea received cuttings from the Tea Development Authority (KTDA) and training in how to plant, prune, and harvest. The KTDA also provided transport; it collected the farmers' crop and delivered it to processing centers. In addition, Kenyatta continued his government's support for settlement schemes in the Rift.

In the years following his assumption of office, Kenyatta continued to back programs to subdivide large farms for settlement by smallholders and the efforts of his wealthy colleagues to promote the resettlement of the landless from Central Province to the Rift.

In the postindependence period, Africa was widely regarded as immersed in a development crisis originating, many argued, from the poor performance of its rural sector. Because its economy continued to grow, Kenya was celebrated as an exception. Singled out for particular praise was its government's vigorous promotion of small holder agriculture.[13]

ZAMBIA

Because Kaunda headed both the party and the government and because members of the Central Committee held seats in the cabinet, should the party choose a political program, that program became government policy. After independence, Zambia had laid claim to the mining revenues that had formerly flowed to the Federation and with the onset of the war

in Vietnam, the price of copper climbed and government revenues grew. Both politically and economically, then, Kaunda was
well positioned to cater to the needs of his core constituency.

As the date for Zambia's first elections drew near, UNIP and
its government began organizing farming cooperatives. Villagers,
it urged, should join together and by registering as a cooperative
qualify for loans from the government. Rather than cash, the
government advanced seeds, fertilizers, pesticides, and services
from a fleet of tractors stationed throughout the rural areas. The
costs of these inputs were then deducted from the proceeds villagers later realized upon the sale of their crop to the government.

Four years later, the second postindependence election
loomed and the party's leaders once again found themselves
accountable to the rural electorate. Once again they championed a rural economic agenda. This time the Central Committee directed the government to increase its investment in the
National Agricultural and Marketing Board (NAMBoard), an
agency charged with distributing "farm inputs"—such as seeds,
fertilizers, pesticides, and such—at the beginning of the agricultural cycle and collecting produce at the end. NAMBoard
had long served farmers along the line-of-rail; the government
now extended its operations to the remoter districts as well. In
addition, the government announced that NAMBoard would
follow a uniform pricing policy; producers now would receive
the same price no matter where they farmed.[14]

Through efforts such as these, Kaunda sought to consolidate
UNIP's hold on the regions that lay off the line-of-rail.

Expanding the Political Base

In the years following independence, Kenyatta and Kaunda
attempted to extend their political reach while also cultivating

their political bases, Central Province and the districts that lay off the line-of-rail, respectively. The impulse to expand did not derive from any simplistic equation of territory with power. Rather it derived from their need to consolidate their hold on their core constituencies. Kenyatta needed access to the Rift in order to resolve the tensions that plagued the Central Province. Kaunda sought to gain power over the Copperbelt in order to lay claim to the resources with which to placate his colleagues atop the ruling party, most of whom were accountable to the poor regions off of the line-of-rail.

KENYA

To consolidate his hold on Central Province, Kenyatta needed to reduce the tensions between the two elements of his political constituency: the wealthy and landed on the one side and the poor and the landless on the other. Mobilizing the public bureaucracy and working with members of the Central Province elite, he sought to placate the former freedom fighters by supplying them with land in the Rift Valley.

Standing between Kenyatta and his goal stood the leaders of the Kenya African Democratic Union (KADU), including one Daniel arap Moi. Among the most senior of Kenya's politicians, Moi had served in the Legislative Assembly since Africans were first allowed to do so; he had helped build and lead KADU, the party that had negotiated Kenya's first constitution.[15] KADU was based upon the smaller and less prosperous ethnic communities. Uniting these groups was the realization that the Kikuyu were far more numerous than they and far richer besides. Though speaking different languages and practicing different customs, these communities united in response to the threat of domination by the denizens of Central Province.

Seeking to counter resistance to his policies, Kenyatta met with the leaders of KADU and offered a political deal: merge your party with mine, he proposed. Better to negotiate from within the governing party than to rail at it from without, he argued. Furthermore, facing no opposition party, those who defected from KADU would have a better chance of retaining their seats. KADU's leaders agreed to accept the offer and Kenya became a one-party state.

In his negotiations with KADU, Kenyatta targeted Moi for special favor. Not only was Moi one of the leaders of the party, he was also the leading spokesman for the Kalenjin in the Rift. To lure Moi into his coalition, Kenyatta made him minister of home affairs. Soon thereafter, he made him vice president, thereby placing him next in the line of succession to the presidency.

By making Moi powerful, Kenya also made him rich. As minister of home affairs, simply by making a phone call, Moi could prevent the boarding of an airplane, freeze a bank account, suspend a license or launch an inspection, and so damage or destroy a firm. As vice president, he could influence the allocation of contracts for vehicles, weapons, clothing, communications, or real estate—contracts that could make the fortunes of a businessman and, through "kickbacks," for himself as well. In either post, he could call for an audit of someone's accounts or for a review of their tax forms. As a result, businessmen found it wise to place Moi's colleagues on their boards or to offer them shares in their firms. Moi was therefore able to squeeze the local business community, which, being dominated by foreigners, was particularly vulnerable to political persuasion. And by diverting a significant portion of this bounty to others, he was able to consolidate his political network.[16] By recruiting his colleagues from the Rift, he was able to forestall opposition to the inmigration of Kikuyu.

Kenyatta had found his man.

ZAMBIA

Kaunda's constituency was the Central Committee of UNIP, which was made up of the old guard who had fought for independence and drew their support from rural regions off the line-of-rail.

To extend his political base, Kaunda had to find a way of gaining access to resources from the richer portions of the country. He did so by marshaling the power of UNIP. Beginning in the late 1960s, he called a series of party conferences and at each announced new economic policies. In the first, he proclaimed that only Zambian citizens could own small businesses and retail firms. At the urging of the governing party, the state then seized a major portion of the commercial sector[17] and transferred it to the hands of African citizens. In the second, Kaunda announced the nationalization of financial firms. In the third, he announced the nationalization of the mines. In the periods between these proclamations came a stream of additional announcements that outlined the structure of Zambia's new economy. At the center stood the government, which, through ZIMCO[18]—a holding company—assumed a controlling interest in the mining industry. Through INDECO,[19] it dominated as well the boards of firms that produced food, clothing, footwear, and other consumer goods. In practice, it was not the state that controlled these holding companies; UNIP's leaders filled the government's seats on the boards. UNIP was thus transformed from a liberation movement to a socialist party. It now controlled the economy of Zambia's richest regions. It had extended its reach from the poorest to the wealthiest regions in Zambia.

To consolidate its hold on these regions, UNIP had to gain backing from the people who lived—and voted—there. In the Copperbelt, which lay in the northern portion of the line-of-rail, that meant gaining the backing of those who worked on the mines.

The Copperbelt

During the independence struggle, the party was able to win support from the mine workers by championing their interests as Africans. It had not been difficult to define labor disputes as racial conflicts, given the composition of the mines' labor force. But in the postindependence era, issues came to the fore that could no longer be defined in this fashion. To consolidate his hold on the poor regions of Zambia, Kaunda, as we have seen, levied resources from the mines to promote programs designed to benefit their farmers. Doing so, he competed with the workers for a share of the mines' revenues. Now that the government owned the companies, there were no third parties on whom to lay blame when the workers felt shortchanged by management.

To assuage such tensions, UNIP continued to subsidize the costs of food. While regarded as prosperous by comparison with rural dwellers, the mine workers were poor by international standards. As do all poor people, they spent a large portion of their income on food, and the price of maize, the staple of most Zambians' diet, was therefore of critical importance to their well-being. For Kaunda to extend his political reach into the Copperbelt, he had to continue to provision the mine townships with affordable produce. And it was mining revenues that enabled Kaunda's government to subsidize the costs of transport, thus enabling the government to supply the Copperbelt with low-cost grain. The political contract between town and country now rested on revenues from the mines. He therefore had to continue to extract revenues from the Copperbelt.

The mine workers now began to notice a decline in the industry: management cut back on prospecting and closed old shafts; machines and equipment grew old; and working conditions became more dangerous. They also saw that their townships were decaying, that services were declining in quality, and that their pensions and benefits were eroding as well. And no longer could UNIP and the mines' labor find common ground by placing the blame on foreign owners of the mines. Tensions therefore grew between UNIP and workers in the Copperbelt.

To survive politically, Kenyatta needed to reconcile the demands of the poor from Central Province with the interests of landholders in the Rift; so great was his need that he made Moi both rich and powerful.[20] As for Kaunda: given the economic geography of Zambia, it was only by seizing resources from the mines that he could bridge the divide between the Copperbelt and the rural periphery. Both leaders needed to straddle regional divides. Both were politically vulnerable.

Changing the Political Game

In this section, we note that both leaders therefore began to modify the structure of their institutions and to add a new element—repression—to their mix of policies. As a result, Zambia and Kenya came to resemble what many now regard as "normal" in the developing world: polities that are authoritarian and nations that, experiencing conflict, remain underdeveloped.

ZAMBIA

It will be recalled that when UNIP first faced its electorate, it had unveiled a program of rural development based on the creation of farming cooperatives. While launched with great fanfare, the program fared poorly. Tractor services arrived late, meaning that fields were neither cleared nor plowed before the arrival of the rains. Seeds and fertilizers were delivered late and often were of the wrong kind or quantity. And NAMBoard, the government's marketing service, often failed to collect the cooperatives' harvest.

When conducting my research in the Luapula Valley, I lived in Kasumpa village. Because of NAMBoard's poor performance, the cooperative in Kasumpa generated little revenue, and the revenue it did generate was insufficient to cover the costs of the goods and services that the government supplied. Rather than prospering, its members were falling into debt—and to the very government they had put in power.[21] Visits to other parts of the Valley confirmed that cooperative societies in other villages were failing as well. The people in Luapula also complained about the state of the roads: they were too dusty in the dry season and too muddy when it rained, they said. They noted that even when the main road was passable, vehicles could not use the feeder roads to get to farms; they had to haul goods by hand or by bicycle. People also derided the dilapidated condition of the village's school and the inoperative state of its well. Above all, they complained about the lack of jobs and their inability to make a living by farming. Indicative of the rising discontent was declining attendance at political rallies, people's growing reluctance to assume offices in the party, and more frequent complaints about the "big men." Those they had sent to the capital, people noted, now rarely returned to the valley. When the "big men" did visit, they quickly retreated back to the city—driven away, it was said, by the mosquitoes. "Our party," people said, "has forgotten us." As confirmed by the work of other scholars, this disillusion became widespread.[22]

UNIP was well aware that those who formed its core were becoming disillusioned. Judging by the results of the elections that followed the achievement of independence, neither the president nor the members of the Central Committee had reason to fear being driven from office. But the declining number of people casting votes in national elections and the declining size of the majorities they secured at the polls gave its leaders pause. They were aware of a growing sense of disillusion within their political base.

Throughout his political career, Kaunda had been, above all else, a political organizer. When he confronted political challenges, rather than launching new policies, he innovated organizationally. It is therefore not surprising that upon noting the rising apathy of his political base, Kaunda altered the rules governing UNIP.

UNIP needed to be "shaken up," he concluded; its office-holders needed to be more strongly motivated to serve the party's members. Rather than being appointed to office, the members of the Central Committee needed instead to compete for them. Motivated by fear for their political fortunes, Kaunda reasoned, they would impart greater dynamism to the government departments over which they presided. They would work harder to mobilize the resources of the government.

When Kaunda introduced electoral competition within the ranks of his party, attention focused on the vice presidency. Whoever became vice president would be well positioned to succeed him as the president of the party; and if UNIP remained the governing party, whoever became vice president could become president of the republic.

During the campaigns for office, two coalitions formed within the ruling party, one led by the sitting vice president, Reuben Kamanga from Eastern Province, and the other led by Simon Kapwepwe, doyen of the delegation from Northern Province—and a Member of Parliament from the Copperbelt. When the votes were tallied, it seemed that Kapwepwe and his coalition had won. But Kamanga and his team fought back. Having long served as vice president, Kamanga had access to multiple networks within the bureaucracy and they fed him, and he the press, stories of corruption and skullduggery by those who had unseated him. Those newly elected, in turn, sought to blacken Kamanga's reputation. Within the townships, rival factions soon formed. Fighting broke out. And civil servants who been posted from Northern Province to serve in Eastern Province—where Kamanga was from—came to fear for their lives and had to be evacuated. In the face of growing discord, Kaunda abandoned his political experiment. He reinstalled Kamanga as deputy president, a move that provoked Kapwepwe to resign from UNIP."[23]

Despite pleas that he return, Kapwepwe refused to do so; instead, he began organizing an opposition party. A quick glance at the electoral geography suffices to reveal the danger Kaunda was then in. Should ANC, the opposition party, hold onto Central and Southern provinces and Kapwepwe's new party triumph in Northern Province, Luapula, and the Copperbelt, UNIP would indeed be in danger of becoming a minority party.[24] Under the rules of the political game, Kaunda could no longer win.

KENYA

Kenyatta too faced growing opposition. Given the structure of the political terrain and the strategy he pursued to conquer it,

Kenyatta also found himself in danger. Kenyatta came from the wealthiest province in Kenya, and he and his family presided over the wealthiest clique within it. He had long championed policies designed to bring prosperity to his core constituency. The result was growing criticism from politicians who charged the president with favoring his own.

Some of the opposition came from outside Central Province, and in particular from Nyanza Province and its energetic leader, Oginga Odinga. Situated far from Nairobi, Nyanza was poor. It was home to mosquito-borne diseases and parasites that were harmful to man and beast and endowed with heavy clay soils, difficult to hoe or plow. While Central Province may have been prospering under Kenyatta's tutelage, Odinga realized, Kenya's other provinces, and most notably his own, were not. Politicians and intellectuals were quick to rally behind Odinga's critique. In the language that was fashionable at the time, they stated that while Kenya's economy may be prospering under Kenyatta, the "center" was diverging from the "periphery" and prosperity was unevenly distributed.[25]

Other criticisms originated from within Kenyatta's home base. There it was Kenyatta's family that provided the focal point for the disaffected. The holdings of this "Royal Family"—in the words of Barry's classic articles[26]—included land in the Rift Valley and coffee farms in the highlands; real estate in Nairobi; and licenses to open gambling saloons, hotels, and game lodges in Central Province and the coast. The conspicuous wealth of the Kenyattas provoked the ire of those who had failed to reap the fruits of independence. In the mid-1960s Odinga ventured forth from Nyanza, joined forces with radical politicians in Central Province, and formed the Kenya People's Union (KPU). The KPU highlighted the growth of inequality in Kenya and championed a socialist alternative to Kenyatta's vision of development.[27]

Opposition to Kenyatta's rule was intensifying. It had spread nationally. As was true with Kaunda, Kenyatta could no longer be sure of winning the political game.

The Presidents Change

In Zambia and Kenya, the politicians atop the political hierarchy were now aware of their political vulnerability. They now realized that they could lose power. We now note how they responded. We begin with Zambia, where the incumbent adopted a new set of strategies and, by changing the institution within which he maneuvered, pruned one path to defeat from the political game tree. We then turn to Kenya, where we find "nature" making the decisive move.

ZAMBIA

Kaunda now realized that he could no longer be sure of winning. When he responded to this threat, he did so by expanding the mix of policies from which he could choose and by altering the institutions in which he maneuvered politically.

Hitherto, Kaunda had largely refrained from using his power to intimidate or repress. He instead presented himself as a "humanist," or someone who used power not to advance an ideology or to pursue material gain but rather to promote human well-being.[28] But in response to Kapwepwe's break with the party, Kaunda no longer acted with restraint; instead he unleashed the coercive powers of the state. He rounded up Kapwepwe and his followers and placed them in jail. Where once Kaunda had chosen to negotiate and to bargain, he now chose to coerce.

In addition, Kaunda altered the institution within which he competed for victory. Zambia had been a republic in which political parties competed for power, with the winner earning the right to form the government. Instead, Kaunda made it a one-party state—with himself at its head. A new constitution enshrined UNIP as the sole legal party and made repeated reference to "the Party and the state." At the opening of Parliament and on other ceremonial occasions, the Central Committee took precedence over the cabinet.

Having reconfigured the setting within which he exercised power, and having shed his reluctance to coerce, Kaunda remained atop the political hierarchy for nearly two more decades. In contrast to other nations in Africa, Zambia remained peaceful. But while Zambia may have achieved security, it declined economically.

A significant part of that decline can be attributed to the impact of neighboring conflicts. As a "front-line state," Zambia paid a high price for the restrictions that it imposed on trade with the white-dominated states on its borders. As an exporter of minerals, it suffered when oil-producing states limited their exports, thereby triggering a global recession. While conceding the importance of such "external" determinants of Zambia's economic performance, those who have studied Zambia stress as well the impact of government policies.[29]

Most who advanced this argument stress the government's overvaluation of the national currency, the kwacha, a policy that enabled the government virtually to confiscate the revenues earned by its mines. When the mines exported copper, they earned foreign exchange. Being owned by the government, they then surrendered foreign "dollars" at a price of the government's choosing. The government persistently chose a rate of exchange that diverged from that which would have prevailed in open markets; it purchased the dollars cheaply. In these—and other—ways, the government extracted resources from the copper mines. While it thereby gained resources with which to finance its efforts to upgrade the lives of those living off the line-of-rail, it deprived the mining industry of much-needed resources. From being one of the most prosperous nations of Africa, with an annual per capita income of nearly $800 at the time of independence, by the end of the century, Zambia had become poor, with an average income of around $400 per annum.[30]

In 1991, Kaunda was driven from power. When viewed from the perspective of this chapter, the events surrounding his political demise emerge laden with meaning.[31] Food riots on the Copperbelt triggered his political demise. With the decline of the mines, the party could no longer manage the tensions between rich region and poor.

KENYA

Unlike Kaunda, Kenyatta had long enjoyed a reputation for violence. While keeping his distance from Mau Mau, he had found it politic to associate himself with the movement and to refrain from publicly condemning its use of violence. And after becoming president, he assembled and staffed "special units"; some he used for the defense of Kenya's borders and others to quell dissent and to intimidate his foes.

The growing wealth of his family put Kenyatta at the center of the controversies surrounding his government's policies and their impact on the nation. The murder of one J. M. Kariuki fixed in people's minds an unflattering image of Kenyatta: not the image of him as a leader of the independence struggle and as a martyr who had been jailed for the sake of the cause but rather as a person who used public power for private gain—and who would, if necessary, be willing to still the voices of those who might protest.

J. M. Kariuki had once served as Kenyatta's secretary. During the colonial period, he had been active in the struggle and been arrested by the British and detained. Released at the end of the state of emergency, he first worked for Kenyatta and then launched a political career of his own. His constituency lay not in Kiambu, the land of the prosperous, but rather in Nyandarua, home to many who had joined the freedom fighters. As Kenyatta's cronies and kin grew richer, Kariuki, like others, grew more critical of his government. When criticizing Kenyatta, J. M., as he was called, did not assume the airs of a village elder, as had Odinga; rather, he played the role of a street-smart young man. As if he were the disappointed offspring of an admired elder, he sharpened his criticisms and made them more personal. Citing evidence drawn from his knowledge of Kenyatta and his family, Kariuki spoke as someone who had been betrayed.

In 1975, Kariuki was shot dead in the streets of Nairobi. Many believe that Kenyatta had him killed. And when Parliament investigated Kariuki's murder, its report listed a series of persons they thought to be "of interest" but could not bring to testify. Among them was Peter Mbiyu Koinange, who now worked in the Office of the President. The family that had invested in Kenyatta's career continued to protect its asset.[32]

Shifting the Regional Base

Had Kenyatta been younger, he, like Kaunda, might also have been able to prolong his hold on power. But in 1978 he died. As a result of his death, Kenya offers us additional data that give insight into the relationship between regionalism and the use of power.

When Kenyatta died, Moi, as vice president, ascended to the top of Kenya's political hierarchy.[33] Power then shifted from Central Province to the Rift. Should our argument be well-founded, then this variation, which is within country, should confirm what we have inferred from cross-national comparisons: that regional characteristics influence the use of power.

Recall the quantity and quality of the public services supplied to the small farmers of Central Province. Shortly after becoming president, Moi unleashed the power of his government upon this infrastructure. His registrar of societies seized and examined the accounts of the cooperative societies; what they could not find, they fabricated, thereby driving many of the staff from office. They harassed and pilloried officials of the Coffee Board, leaking inflated estimates of their salaries to the press. These measures led to the seizure of the funds of the cooperatives in Central Province and to their transfer to banks that served cooperatives in western Kenya, Moi's core constituency.

Under Moi, the government continued to intervene in the maize industry and to suffer large losses as a result. As would any other president, Moi feared the rage of Nairobi's consumers; but the large farmers that formed so significant a portion of Kenyatta's core constituency lay outside Moi's own. Rather, his ties were with the small maize farmers. To solidify his hold on these farmers, upon assuming power, Moi ordered the construction of hundreds of "local buying centers" throughout the valley. He forged institutional ties between his rural constituents and the urban market.

Kenyatta came to power as the visible and capable face of a family whose roots penetrated deep into the fabric of Central Province. He used his position atop the central hierarchy to promote the prosperity of his region and his family and to defend both against those who might threaten it. When power shifted from Central Province to the Rift, these defenses were breached and resources began to flow to its residents.

An Additional Shock

The death of Kenyatta thus shocked the political system and, by moving the president's base, altered the political game. Little more than a decade later, another shock followed: the end of the Cold War.

As had Kaunda and Kenyatta, Moi too faced political criticism. In Nairobi, a university town and the national capital, crowds often demonstrated against his government and demanded political reform. Moi's critics at home were joined by his creditors abroad in calling for political change. International financial institutions had come to believe that poor public policies lay at the roots of Africa's poverty and that only by rendering governments accountable to their people could these policies be changed. The route to economic reform therefore ran through political reform, they believed. The institutions that held Kenya's debt therefore began to join with the government's domestic critics and to press for political change. Moi had preserved Kenyatta's single-party system. Local activists and international creditors now called for Moi to allow opposition parties to compete for power.

On November 9, 1989, the Berlin Wall fell and throughout the globe things changed. Because Kenya was located on the Indian Ocean, Western powers had long considered the country a strategic asset. With the end of the Cold War, however, its value to the West declined and Western governments therefore allowed financial institutions to intensify their efforts to secure political change. Indeed, they encouraged their embassies to back those in Kenya who were demanding the reintroduction of competitive elections.

As Kenya's value to Western security declined, Moi's bargaining position weakened. After long and often unpleasant negotiations, he determined that he had no alternative but to change the political rules. In 1991, opposition parties therefore again became legal in Kenya.

Recall Kenya's political terrain: the Kikuyu had settled about Mt. Kenya and the Kalenjin-speaking peoples in the Rift. Some in Central Province—and especially in Kiambu—had become rich and had promoted the migration of the poor and landless to the Rift. Those "native to" the valley remained opposed to further inmigration. Within this setting, the reintroduction of electoral competition proved inflammatory.

In the run-up to the elections, politicians first competed to be chosen as a candidate. On the side of the politicians from Central Province, this meant posing as a sponsor of migrants and as a defender of their claims to land. On the side of those from the Rift—which included Moi—it meant competing to be seen as the defender of locals who feared the loss of land. Once chosen as candidates, the politicians then strove to deliver the benefits they had promised. In the Rift, politicians purchased and distributed weapons, leased vehicles for purposes of combat, and organized the invasion of settlements, the burning of homes, and the slaughter of families. After the reintroduction of electoral competition into Kenya's politics, repression gave way to violence.[34]

In both Kenya and Zambia, the nature and quality of the politics we observe reveal the influence of the terrain within which the political game was played. In Zambia, to survive politically, politicians used power in a way that undermined the wealth of the nation. In Kenya, they used it in ways that cost the lives of thousands. In both, the way they used power undermined their nation's development.

Envoi

I began our examination of today's developing world by taking the reader to Kasumpa, a village two days north of Zambia's Copperbelt, in the northern portions of Luapula Province. From time to time, I have returned there, seeking thereby to recenter my argument on observations made in the field rather than on materials drawn from scholarly works.

One of the most important things I learned is that while people who live in the agrarian periphery may be poor, they are crafty. To see just how crafty, return to figure 4.6, which provides a "light map" of Zambia. Cones rise from the Copperbelt and the capital city, indicating where productive activity has spurred the consumption of electrical power. These cones are then surrounded by regions from which no light rises, save for one: a small cone that rises from Luapula. As Zambia's economy declined, it appears, Luapula gained.

Investigation reveals that when Kapwepwe competed for the post of vice president in UNIP, others labeled him a "Bemba politician," thereby branding him as a tribalist. After negotiating with Kapwepwe, however, a delegation from Luapula endorsed his candidacy, referring to him not as a Bemba but as a "Northerner" like themselves. For Kapwepwe's démarche to succeed, he needed to add an additional province to his coalition and took aim at the Copperbelt. Politicians from Luapula again backed his initiative, this time characterizing his coalition as "Bemba speaking."

The Luapulaists then pivoted. Backing away from Kapwe-pwe, they then turned to the president. For far too long, they stated, they had been treated as an appendage of Kapwepwe's faction; they now wanted to be dealt with directly. They had interests of their own.[35]

As events unfolded, rather than defecting with Kapwepwe, they instead stayed with Kaunda. But for a price. The light map reveals the power of their tactics. The road that runs the full length of the valley was upgraded; a refrigeration facility for the fisheries now graces the shores of Lake Meru; and a power plant provides electricity for the plant and light for the lake-shore township. Luapula's wily politicians thus secured what every region desired: public investments.

7

Conclusion

How does the use of power shape the process of development? In search of materials with which to address this question, I—as have others—turned to the developing world. Those who study that world speak of convergence; they measure development by the degree to which the per capita incomes of its residents come to approximate those in advanced industrial societies. But by this criterion, only a handful of countries can be said to have developed: Korea, Japan, Hong Kong, Taiwan, Singapore, and arguably five or so more.[1] These "success cases" are few in number and most come from the same region of the world. They therefore comprise a sample that contains little information and so can tell us little about how development is achieved.[2]

Some may object, noting that more people have moved out of poverty in the last several decades than in any previous period; that the developing world has recently witnessed the rise of a large middle class; and that the global distribution of income has therefore improved. But note that the data that engender this response are based on the incomes of individuals.

When we instead use the nation as the unit of account we find that what at first appeared to be a global improvement is largely the product of changes in but two countries with large—indeed massive—populations: India and China. The problem I address is the performance of nations, and most nations have failed to develop.

The Turn to History

Given my goal, I therefore faced a problem: I could not understand development, much less the role of politics in achieving it, by studying the developing world. In response to this problem, I turned to the past and to cases drawn from history.

More specifically, I turned to Europe when it too was poor, agrarian, and underdeveloped. There I focused on two cases, England and France. In key respects, they were similar: for much of the period under study, their residents worshipped the same God, spoke the same language, paid homage to the same dynasties, and fought over common territory. And yet at the end of the eighteenth century, England entered the Great Transformation while France descended into political violence. One became prosperous and secure; in the other, prosperity was delayed and violence engulfed the lives of its citizens. By the criteria adopted here, in the late eighteenth century, England began to develop whereas France failed to do so. The two cases offered a point of entry into my study of the role of politics in the process of development.

Because I wished to apply what I could learn from these cases to development in the modern era, I focused my attention on a common set of variables; thus box 1.1, which enumerates the features that characterize agrarian societies. When I put this template to use, however, I was soon struck by the importance of factors that I had overlooked when creating it. In particular, I quickly grasped the significance of regions: subnational centers of culture, wealth, and power. Long conditioned to think of Absolutism as absolute and France as "statist" and therefore unitary, I was surprised by the degree to which the nation's politics was shaped by its regions. In France, regions were powerful; indeed, they were so powerful that they shaped the manner in which those at the center employed their power.

Upon reflection, I realized that regions are an emergent property; they are the product of factors embedded in my notion of an agrarian society. As rural dwellers seek to elude the impact of diminishing returns, they migrate. When doing so, they take with them their cultural practices, including their laws; and when they settle, they continue to abide by local law and custom. Once settled, they begin to specialize, growing or making goods in the production of which they hold a relative advantage and trading what they produce for products made by others. Becoming economically distinctive as well, their members come to share common interests; they become politically distinctive as well. Regions thus "emerge" as a product of the law of diminishing returns and the attempts of families to mitigate its impact through migration, specialization, and trade.

Materials from France suggest that, when faced with powerful regions, those atop the central political hierarchy seek to intimidate; they appear to judge proclamations and ultimata as more productive than attempts at cooperation. Materials from England suggest that regionalism was less significant there. The legal system was "common"; the Conquest had put paid to regional centers of power, and the interests of powerful families were national rather than regional in scope. The monarch in England appears to have found it more useful to consult and to elicit than to issue ultimata and therefore appeared weak by comparison with his counterpart in France. But by teaming with other members of the political class, he mobilized collective efforts in pursuit of common objectives and therefore became the more powerful. The English monarch was better able than the monarch in France to mobilize support for his efforts to enrich and to strengthen the polity he governed. The presence of regionalism in the one case and its relative absence in the other thus helped explain differences in the manner in which their monarchs governed.

The Political Roots of Contemporary Development

When I turned to the developing world, I soon realized that it resembled France to a far greater degree than it resembled England. The "laws of motion" that shaped the behavior of imperialist states had led to the acquisition of "too much" territory, that is, of holdings too numerous and too large to be governed directly. The imperial states therefore found it preferable to recruit local confederates and to devolve power upon them. The result was the creation of polities that resembled aggregates: collections of smaller units forcefully assembled and then released upon the world when their masters could no longer afford them. In much of the developing world, then, regionalism prevails. It characterizes the political terrain.

To assess how that terrain shapes the use of power, I turned to Zambia and Kenya and those who first governed them. Both Kaunda and Kenyatta, I noted, confronted a similar problem: to consolidate their hold on the central hierarchy, each had first to secure his political base and then to extend his political reach into other regions of his polity. In the case of Kenyatta, to secure his natal constituency, he had to curry favor with its elite while also promoting the fortunes of the *wanachi*. Thus his use of

power to enrich his friends, giving them access to loans, award-
ing them contracts, or granting them lucrative licenses; thus
too his backing of agricultural programs, which enriched the
lives and fortunes of the province's smallholders. But given the
regional structure of Kenya's political terrain, Kenyatta could
not placate a third member of his constituency—the landless—
without the cooperation of those living in the Rift. By law and
custom, the lands he needed belonged to those who dwelled
there; and those who competed for political office within the
Rift had no choice but to oppose his resettlement program. In
Zambia, Kaunda's region was sectoral; he competed for ascen-
dancy within UNIP, a party whose roots lay in the poorer rural
districts that lay off the line-of-rail. But he found it difficult to
extend his reach to the Copperbelt, which contained the indus-
trialized portions of the country. The Copperbelt had backed
him in the liberation struggle; but as the fiscal burden of his
programs rose and the productivity of the mines diminished,
it turned against him, thus threatening his grasp on power.

In Zambia as in Kenya, then, regional differences made it
difficult for those competing for power at the national level to
take the steps necessary to secure their positions atop the central political hierarchy. They found it difficult to satisfy those
who constitute their political base on the one hand while extending their political reach on the other. In both instances, it therefore proved difficult to form a national team in support of collective objectives—such as development.

Shaping the Political Game

So how, in such a setting, do politicians behave? They continue to compete for positions atop the political hierarchy. But
when those atop it feel unable to assure themselves of victory,

they change the political game. From our study of Zambia and Kenya, we learn that they do so in at least three ways.

AUTHORITARIAN POLITICS

In regionally segmented societies, political delegations compete for rewards from the center; regional elites compete for projects. Politics then becomes a "divide the dollar" game, as political leaders from each region seek to capture the largest possible share of the government's expenditures.[3] As politicians have long known and scholars long ago proved, when political competition takes this form, no coalition can be assured of "winning."[4] Political competition therefore gives rise to political uncertainty.

If only because the struggle for benefits erodes the value of the payoffs from the game, competitors come to prefer the assured provision of a small reward to the remoter prospect of the large payoff that results from winning. In environments rife with distributional struggles, members of the political class come to accede to the creation of an authoritarian regime; they accede to the rule of a "big man" with the power to put an end to unbridled competition. This was the case in Zambia and Kenya. It is true elsewhere as well. While in the developed portions of the globe, competitive political systems far outnumber authoritarian regimes, in the developing world, authoritarian regimes are common.[5]

PRIVATE BENEFITS

The political terrain shapes the use of power in another way: it leads to a preference for private, and therefore targetable, payoffs as opposed to public, and therefore non-excludable, benefits. People conceive of development as a public good, but it comes in discrete packages: education requires schools; health care requires clinics; and sanitation requires wells and clean water. Budgets are limited, however, and in any given period, some but not all districts receive projects. As a result, some politicians will "win": they will gain politically from having brought "development" to their region. But the standing of others will decline; they will be seen as having failed to provide comparable benefits.

Those atop the political hierarchy therefore find disaffection arising within the ranks of those who may once have supported them. To forestall the spread of opposition, the leaders compensate those whose political careers they have put in danger by conferring upon them private benefits.[6] Thus did Kenyatta enrich Moi and Moi enrich his colleagues in the Rift. So too do others; they distribute cash, jobs, permits, or licenses, thereby seeking to forestall opposition from those whose districts have been ignored.

Authoritarianism and corruption: both can be seen as products of political competition in settings marked by regional diversity.[7]

VIOLENCE

As politicians compete for places atop the political hierarchy, we witness as well the use of violence. Both Moi and Kaunda, it will be noted, confronted attempted coups; in both Kenya and Zambia, urban riots broke out; and in Kenya, local politicians organized pogroms to rid the Rift of Kikuyu settlers. Political violence is more likely in the developing world than in the developed.[8] To understand why, it is useful to turn from the politicians and how they use power and to focus instead on their constituents.

Recall that in agrarian societies, families confront the law of diminishing returns and many seek to elude its impact by choosing to migrate. Recall too that in the Luapula Valley, those who left were young; that the older generation prepared the young to depart by paying for their education; and the older generation subsequently benefited, as the youths remitted a portion of their earnings to their elders.

A similar story could be told of Nigeria, where people in the Eastern Region migrated to Lagos, the national capital; to Ibadan in the Western Region; and to Kano and Kaduna in the North.[9] It could be told as well about South Asia, where villagers flocked to cities in India, Pakistan, Malaysia, and elsewhere.[10] Families search for prosperity not only by moving from to town; many move from one rural area to another. Some move from grasslands to forests, which they clear and burn in order to raise livestock or to grow crops. Best known, perhaps, is the felling of forests in Indonesia and Brazil. Others move from lowlands to highlands in search of greater moisture. Thus the change in settlement patterns in Darfur and Ethiopia.

Migration can lead to violence. As we have seen, such was the case in the Rift. Such was also the case in Nigeria, where locals drove immigrants from the cities in northern and western Nigeria, slaughtering them in the process. And in South and Southeast Asia, conflicts between immigrants and sons of the soil have long inflamed politics.[11] Immigrants compete for land and jobs. And by altering the composition of the electorate, they pose a threat to those in power.[12] In either fashion, migrants pose threats and migration therefore increases the likelihood of violence.

The search for prosperity not only takes the form of spatial mobility; it takes the form of vertical mobility as well. And this form of mobility too gives rise to political dangers.

When a child appears forceful or studious or clever, family members may decide to invest in the child's education. If found promising, the parents will seek to provide him more than a mere primary education; they may search for enough funds to provide a secondary education or even a college degree. For many families, the costs exceed their ability to pay, and they therefore turn to other members of the community. As the biographies of those who have benefited from such efforts make clear, if not legally in debt to those who backed them, they feel a sense of moral obligation; they feel a need to repay those who have made possible their good fortune. The accounts suggest as well that their sponsors are not shy about demanding repayment, some in the form of material compensation and others in the form of public service.[13]

When conflicts arise between communities, the news disseminates from the point of conflict to "home." And because of the ties forged between rural communities and the elite they have forged, the hue and cry then resonates through the professions, the universities, and the government bureaucracy. Those who occupy posts in these institutions are then called upon to use their positions to aid those at home.[14]

In regionally diverse polities, national institutions are staffed with people deeply obligated to their communities. And when sons of the soil attack immigrants, or when migrants are driven from urban townships, or when politicians organize the defense of their community and mobilize it to secure their hold on power, institutions that were once crafted to pursue collective objectives are then weakened or torn asunder.

As noted by the State Failure Task Force and others, violence becomes particularly likely when one community is large enough and powerful enough to seize the state. Those excluded from power then find their customs and legal systems under threat; they and those they love face the possibility of permanent exclusion. The value of future payoffs then turns negative. The alternative—resistance—though perilous, offers at least the possibility of positive gains. Those driven from power therefore become willing to rebel. Thus too can the political terrain affect the decisions that shape the use of power.[15]

In political terrains marked by regional diversity, the pursuit of prosperity can thus lead to conflict. Institutions that were forged to promote the agenda of the nation may be fractured or diverted to the service of sectional interests. Under the conditions set out above, regionalism can turn into violence. In this way too does the political terrain in the developing world shape the use of power.

The Broader Setting

In this work, I address the use of power in the developing world. Doing so, I follow in the footsteps of those who pioneered the study of such development: David Apter, Crawford Young, James Coleman, and others.[16] I approach the topic in a different manner, however. Rather than depicting subnational communities as actors in their own right, I instead focus on the behavior of politicians. In regionally variegated settings, when competing for power, they must consolidate their regional base while striving to gain allies in others. Because this proves difficult to achieve, they change the rules of the political game and alter the way in which they use power. Many become authoritarian, venal, and violent. My predecessors and I may concur regarding the importance of subnational communities, but I look more closely at how they impact the choices made by those with power.

I also follow in the footsteps of the radical generation of political economists who, as do I, probe the politics of the "agrarian periphery."[17] I depart from these scholars, however, in that I stress the importance of internal rather than international forces when accounting for their underdevelopment. Imperialism may have fashioned these countries, I contend, but its debilitating impact operates not only through international markets and trade but also through the structural legacy that it bequeathed to countries in the developing world: a political terrain shaped by the forces of regionalism.

My arguments resonate as well with those of Samuel Huntington.[18] Like Huntington, I put the use of power at the core of my argument. As does Huntington, I emphasize the importance of political order and see violence as the product of efforts to develop. And like Huntington, I stress the importance of institutions. Where we differ is in how we approach these subjects. I make greater use of history and use the past to gain insight into today's developing nations. While Huntington addresses the conduct of macro-aggregates—sectors, institutions, and parties—I operate at the microlevel and focus on farmers, families, and politicians.[19] And while Huntington treats institutions as definers and defenders of the public interest, I view them as implementing the preferences of those who sit atop them: the winners of the political game. By my account, the central question then becomes: In the competition to preside over political institutions, which strategies will prove winning: using their power to promote the growth of prosperity by securing life and property or using it to seize and redistribute wealth?

My analysis also intersects with recent works in economic history, such as those by North and Wallis et al. and Acemoglu and Robinson.[20] North and Wallis et al. distinguish between "open-access" societies whose institutions promote Schumpeterian growth and "natural societies" whose institutions do not. Acemoglu and Robinson distinguish between "strong" and "weak" institutions; by strong, they mean institutions capable of checking the predatory use of power, and by weak, those incapable of doing so. All that I have written here underscores my debt to these scholars; but it also highlights what distinguishes their work from my own. Put short, I want to ground my arguments on the analysis of politics. Institutions are created by politicians, after all; and if they are powerful, then it is because politicians delegate power to them.[21] The key issue, then, is not whether institutions are strong or weak or "open-access" or not but rather the conditions under which politicians, while seeking to survive politically, choose to make them so.

Lastly, I hope that this work will resonate with those who have re-created the field of political geography.[22] Scholars such as Cederman and Gleditsch et al. characterize the developing world; they too map out its "political terrain." While I have used narratives to do so, they make systematic use of quantitative data. I hope that the ideas I have exposited are of sufficient interest that in the future political geographers will use their methods to explore them.

Envoi

Throughout the developing world, politicians call for development. But the choices they make appear to be motivated less by the desire for collective improvement than by the need for political survival. Tensions arise from migration and disputes between immigrants and sons of the soil; from regional inequality and the fear and envy to which it gives rise; and from disputes that arise from differences in the laws that govern marriage, inheritance, and the family. Those who aspire to positions atop the political hierarchy would be unwise to ignore such issues. Should they not address them, others surely will, thereby placing them at a political disadvantage. The need for political survival trumps the long-term interest in development.

The result is political instability, and instability is costly. Data confirm that the rate of growth of per capita incomes declines over 3 percentage points following an "irregular" political exit (such as a coup) and by over 9 percentage points following the onset of state failure. Riots, demonstrations, and civil wars: these, too, significantly lower the rate of economic growth.[23] Most important for this argument: the data confirm that these forms of instability occur more frequently in low-income societies than in those that are prosperous.[24]

By way of closing, it is useful to illustrate the implication of these findings. To do so, compare the economic performance of two countries: one politically stable and the other not. Let both start with economies of the same size and let both grow at an *average* of 5 percent a year. But let the economy of one grow steadily and the other erratically,[25] the result of political instability and conflict. The growth of the first is steady, while that in the second surges and declines. When the latter economy grows, it does so in spurts.

Some might be attracted by the high rates of growth occasionally attained by the second economy. But calculations confirm that after five decades the slow but steady growth of the first would lead to incomes *one-sixth* larger than those in its counterpart and that gap will grow greater over time.

As seen in the addendum to this chapter, erratic growth, as in the second economy, marks the developing world. So too does conflict. For development to take place, both prosperity and security are required. But the data suggest that the search for prosperity remains in tension with the search for security. Rather than an achievement, then, for many, development remains an aspiration.

ADDENDUM TO CHAPTER 2

Development is marked by the growth of prosperity and security.[1] The more development increases the more society benefits from both. I contend, however, that with decentralized control of the means of coercion, development is difficult to achieve. Consider the following argument:

Assume that there are two actors:

$$\text{Actors: } i \in (i,j)$$

and that they control:

$$w, \text{work;}$$

$$l, \text{leisure;}$$

and

$$m, \text{military capabilities.}$$

Subject to the constraint Time $= w + l + m$, they seek to maximize their utility, U, which is a function of income (Y) and leisure (L), where $Y_i = f(w_i) + g(m_i)f(w_j)$. That is, Y_i, the income of i, consists of the product of his labor, $f(w_i)$, and his military might, $g(m_i)$, which he can employ to prey upon the earnings of the other player, $f(w_j)$, or to defend the fruits of his labors.

For any reasonable set of payoffs, the interaction between players i and j yields a prisoners' dilemma game. Choosing rationally, both players will use force. But at best the use of force redistributes wealth; it does not create it. And invariably, it diverts time and effort from productive activity. As a result, when the actors choose force, they make themselves worse off than they would were they to refrain from the use of arms.

Thus far I have analyzed the game as if it were to last but a single period. But as many readers will realize, if there were repeated interactions, i and j could achieve higher payoffs.[2] For, given repeated interaction, players can employ contingent strategies. Those who stand to become victims of predation can threaten to retaliate; and, if large enough in size and long enough in duration, the magnitude of the losses they could inflict would outweigh the gains from predation (see figure A.1). When there is repeated play, the actors can therefore avoid being drawn into unproductive interactions.

Once again, let the players repeatedly interact, but now let there be development. Given development, as prosperity increases, then so too do the benefits from predation. And the benefits from the opportunistic appropriation of wealth might then exceed the expected losses from future punishments (compare figures A.1 and A.2).

If the means of coercion are controlled by private agents, there is an inherent tension between prosperity and security and development is difficult to attain.

Second-Best Solutions: The Contradiction Reemerges

The difficulty of combining prosperity with security becomes even more apparent when we abandon the search for "first-best" solutions and look instead at second-best outcomes: one where people maximize the prospects for peace and another where they maximize prosperity.

What we then find is that for $m = 0$ (i.e., peace) to be in equilibrium, people must increase the amount of time they spend

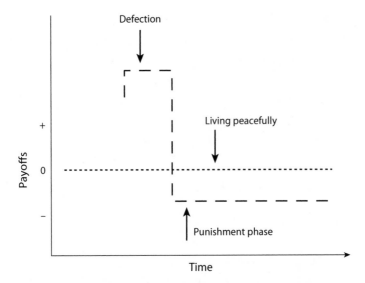

FIGURE A.1. Present benefits, future losses. If future losses are not heavily discounted, they may outweigh the immediate benefits from predation, thus making opportunistic defection unattractive.

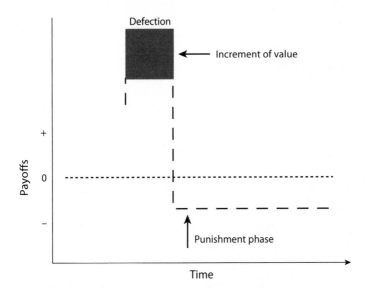

FIGURE A.2. Present benefits and future losses, but with development. When development increases the level of prosperity, the benefits of defection increase. Future losses may then no longer engender restraint.

in leisure. Put another way, they must possess little worth steal-ing. On the other hand, for someone to be prosperous, she must sacrifice leisure for military activity. She must be prepared to fight in order to defend her income.

In societies in which private agents—individuals or families or groups of kin—control the means of coercion, the tension between prosperity and peace runs deep.

Introducing a Central Hierarchy

As seen in figure A.3, the political order analyzed thus far leaves people worse off than they might otherwise prefer. As captured in the line connecting point 1 (wherein society is peaceful but poor) and point 2 (wherein society is prosperous but milita-rized), the best outcomes attainable lie below the ideal point (where people enjoy both prosperity and security).

The line connecting equilibria 1 and 2 can be thought of as a constraint—one imposed by the properties of their institu-tions. People's prospects are constrained because the means of violence remain in private hands. For that reason, I have argued, societies supported the introduction of a central hierarchy and charged it with the task of defending the peace and providing "justice," or ways of settling disputes.

I offer one last diagram (figure A.4). The triangle is the space of outcomes available to the two actors, i and j. Should i and j persist in quarreling, their payoffs would decline to the lowest point of the triangle. While both would prefer to reside on the "efficiency frontier," given the incentives that shape their choices (those of the prisoners' dilemma), they are unable to do so.

For this reason, they may agree to the introduction of a third party (as depicted by the circle in the upper right of the diagram). By abolishing the use of arms and providing peaceful

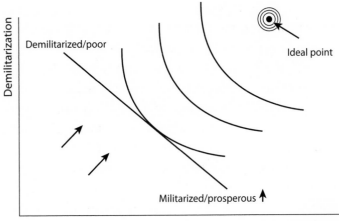

FIGURE A.3. Institutional constraints on attainable levels of well-being. Welfare increases with higher levels of peace and prosperity.

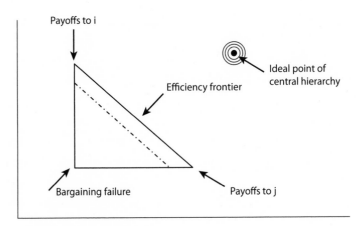

FIGURE A.4. Central enforcement.

forms of dispute settlement, this third party could transform the payoffs of the game; no longer being trapped in a prisoners' dilemma, i and j could bargain and reach settlements lying close to the efficiency frontier. More accurately, by paying tribute or taxes to someone capable of preventing them from taking up arms, i and j become safer and more prosperous than they would have been when they controlled the means of coercion.

The central challenge of development is to secure prosperity *and* security. While this "solution" to the problem may appeal, it is difficult to implement. Once in control of the means of coercion, what is to keep the third party from extracting the entire "surplus" within the bargaining set?[3] Even after the creation of a central hierarchy, development remains difficult to achieve.

ADDENDUM TO CHAPTER 6

I have suggested that the challenges to development in the postimperial world more closely resemble those that shaped the rise of France than those that shaped the rise of England. When making this claim, I have stressed the political significance of regions and, in particular, the importance of regional inequality—a factor that elicits efforts to achieve economic redistribution. But ethnicity and culture also shape relationships between regions, and I therefore now address them.

According to Weber and those who follow him, ethnic groups are made up of people who have shared in the experience of migration. Their escape from oppression, the rigors they endured while in passage, and their safe arrival in their new homeland: such narratives come to form a major part of their cultural heritage.[1] Certainly, all we know about the ethnic groups in Zambia and Kenya would underscore the validity of this claim.[2] But when do heritages or traditions become politicized? Originally, I suggest, it is when disputes arise over land; and as nations form, it is when people bargain over the costs and benefits of government programs. When material and cultural differences overlay each other, then those who occupy different regions begin to think in terms of "us" and "them" and to see that they and their neighbors share not only a common heritage but also a common political position.

To cite but one example, consider the Kalenjin. As noted by Sutton, those we now refer to as the Kalenjin previously consisted of a cluster of different groups, the Nandi, the Kipsigis, the Pokot, and the Tugen among them. After settling in the Rift, they began to cooperate in order to repel cattle raids by the Maasai and then, less successfully, to counter incursions by Europeans. Already aware that they shared linguistic commonalities, they became aware of their common economic interests as well. It was when Kenya was transitioning to independence that they allied and began to call themselves Kalenjin; and it was conflict over land rights with migrants to the Rift that led to this alliance.[3]

Migration, settlement, and conflict: these shape the emergence of ethnic identities. For many readers, this argument may not go far enough. For while it may account for the incidence of ethnic politics, it does not account for the intensity. It is not just interests that are at stake, they will point out, but also notions of honor and identity.

Responding to this critique, I focus once again on the family and on materials drawn from Kenya.

Recall the "model" that appeared in the previous chapter: one in which the family forms a compact between generations. Within that framework, people look forward: the young people are preparing for their entry into the labor market and the working-age population are preparing for their retirement.

It is perhaps for that reason that when I was working in Kenya in the late 1980s, I found both the young and working-aged transfixed by a court case pitting one Wambui Otieno, the wife of the recently deceased Silvanus Melea Otieno (or S. M. as he was known), against a group of elders from Siaya in the Nyanza Province. The issue was: Who had the right to bury S. M.?[4] Both Wambui and S. M. held professional degrees; both had long lived in cosmopolitan Nairobi and frequently traveled abroad. Wambui sought to bury her husband in the national capital; the cemetery was based at a church attended by some of the leading figures in law, business, and politics in Kenya. But while she was a Kikuyu, S. M. was a Luo and the elders from Siaya sought to bury him at home. Throughout Nairobi, where I was working at the time, I found all, but especially the young, transfixed by the trial and by the central question to which it gave rise. To which arena should they aspire: the national or the regional, the metropolitan or the parochial? In which world did their future lie and for which should they prepare?

In many ethnic communities, there are those with the power to preside over the ceremonies that govern passage through the life cycle. They therefore acquire the power to adjudicate claims to titles and to property; to rule on the legitimacy of marriages; and to influence, many believe, the possibility of repose in the afterlife. Their decisions affect the future of all who live in their community.

Another example from Kenya highlights the power of those who preside over the life cycle and, by so doing, establishes a link between ethnicity and politics. The illustration comes from Michela Wrong's study of the government of Mwai Kibaki.[5] Kibaki had assumed the presidency of Kenya following Moi's departure from office. Members of his government were suspected of corruption and of having inflicted truly staggering losses on Kenya's treasury. Kenya's creditors insisted on the appointment of an investigator, and it is he—the late John Githongo—upon whom Wrong focuses. Like President Kibaki, Githongo was a Kikuyu; so too were those he was investigating. In the tension-riven politics of Kenya, he faced pressures— some subtle and insidious, others blatant and sharp edged—to curtail his efforts and to temper his investigation so as to protect "his" president and "his" people. What does this "his" mean and where does it come from, Wrong wonders. Quoting one of Githongo's colleagues, Wrong takes us closer to an answer:

> As you get older, entering into a marriage and having children seems to tribalize you. All those ceremonies, marriage arrangements, land issues: those decisions . . . they activate something in people they didn't know they had.[6]

The spatial distribution of settlement; political conflict over land and power; and local control over the definition of the family—an institution that bridges time and controls access to the future—these features of agrarian societies help imbed and institutionalize ethnicity, rendering it a substantial force in developing societies and many times multiplying the power of regionalism.

Note that this discussion also helps us understand why lineages, while often championing parochial interests in the developing world, were able to preside over nations in Europe. In much of the developing world, the marriage market is subnational in extent; its range is circumscribed by ethnicity. In Europe, by contrast, the market is national—indeed, international. The difference in their reach reflects, I believe, the nature of the marriage market. Because the Catholic Church assumed control over life-cycle rituals and transformed them into sacraments, people from different regions and peoples could marry.[7]

In the developing world, as we have seen, parochial figures, based in regions, preside over the law of the family and so rule on the legitimacy of claims to wealth (i.e., inheritance) and power (i.e., succession). Politically ambitious families are therefore more likely to preside over regions than over nations. The political ambitions of families are more likely to energize regional conflicts than to promote national unity.

The role of the church in regulating marriage in premodern Europe and the importance of elders, ritualists, and kin in the developing world: historians and ethnographers have previously shed light on both. By viewing them together, we deepen our understanding of the politics of development.

ADDENDUM TO CHAPTER 7

In this book, I have mixed argument with case material. Such an approach is likely to leave readers wondering whether the argument may hold in general or simply fit the cases from which it was drawn. I address such concerns here.

To convince the reader of the general applicability of my argument, I could have added additional vignettes: the history of political dynasties in the developing world; tales of the struggles between rich regions and poor; or narratives of public unrest, military coups, and economic decline. Adding further examples would add to the bulk of the manuscript, however; to counter this effect, each account would have had to have been brief—and therefore unconvincing. I therefore turn to the use of numerical data.

Generalizing from Kenya and Zambia

When applying the insights garnered from history to the contemporary world, I addressed Kenya and Zambia. But can Kenya and Zambia "stand in" for the developing world?

Using the size of the agrarian sector as our measure of development, I find that the sectoral composition of their national incomes falls within the interquartile range for developing countries.[1] In Zambia and Kenya, both the percent of GDP originating from agriculture and the percent of the labor force employed in farming are "typical" of the developing world;

they fall within the interquartile range for states that once were colonies.[2]

Shifting our focus from the two countries' economies to their "political terrains," we find that both exhibit "high" levels of ethnic fractionalization and regional inequality; so too do the majority—over 50 percent—of the countries in the developing world. We find that Zambia but not Kenya exhibits a high level of ethnic polarization; in that respect, Zambia is but Kenya is not typical of the developing world.[3] And we find that both countries scored higher than was typically the case among former colonies in Hariri's index of indirect rule.[4]

In most instances, then, the values of the "causal" variables that I have used in this book fall within the normal range of values for all developing nations. The arguments I advance in my case studies should therefore "travel" throughout much of the developing world.

Assessing the Argument

Information extracted from the numerical data suggests that the line of argument advanced in the case studies should apply widely. We can start with data on political instability.

Compared to countries in the developed world, those in the developing world are insecure. Table A.1 informs us that over the period 1966–2012, countries that had formerly been colonies were significantly more likely than were those that had not to have succumbed to state failure and civil war and to have experienced "irregular" transfers of power.[5] Table A.1 also confirms that countries that exhibit regional inequality and high levels of ethnic polarization are more likely to have experienced civil wars and state failure.[6]

TABLE A.1. Political Instability, 1966–2012

	Number of Country Years[c]	High Frequency of Riots, Demonstrations[d]	Irregular Transfers of Power[e]	Civil Wars[f]	State Failure[g]
Colonies[a]	4,746	30.11%	4.16%	13.57%	2.06%
Non-Colonies	2,497	34.00%	2.64%	7.59%	0.77%
		$p = 0.001$	$p = 0.007$	$p = 0.000$	$p = 0.000$
Regional Inequality = Yes	3,710	32.91%	3.51%	16.22%	1.81%
Regional Inequality = No	3,533	29.92%	3.79%	6.69%	1.31%
		$p = 0.000$	$p = 0.336$	$p = 0.000$	$p = 0.023$
High Ethnic Polarization[b]	2,649	28.37%	3.97%	15.85%	2.01%

(continued)

TABLE A.1. (*continued*)

	Number of Country Years[c]	High Frequency of Riots, Demonstrations[d]	Irregular Transfers of Power[e]	Civil Wars[f]	State Failure[g]
Low Ethnic Polarization	2,697	27.29% $p = 0.387$	3.76% $p = 0.774$	11.74% $p = 0.000$	1.01% $p = 0.005$

Note: Countries with the measure of ethnic polarization > +0.5 are rated high. So too are those whose measure of indirect rule is >=0. Data on regional inequality were gathered from data compiled by William Nordhaus and his colleagues (http://gecon.yale.edu) from photographs of the earth taken at night by satellites that record the intensity of artificial light. The intensity of the illumination, they contend, provides a measure of urbanization and energy use, and thus the extent of economic development. Countries judged by a panel of undergraduate researchers as exhibiting pronounced regional differences in the intensity of "night lights" were classified in the first group (labeled "Yes"); others were placed in the second. The ethnic polarization variable is based on the configuration of the size distribution of subnational groups and has repeatedly been found to be significantly related to political conflict. By this measure, the more a nation's population is gathered into a bipolar and symmetrical distribution of ethnic groups, the higher the level of polarization.

[a] Countries that were colonies at any point between 1800 and 2000, excluding Australia, Canada, and New Zealand.

[b] The measure of polarization is divided into high and low at the median. Significance levels are based on the chi-square statistic, save when cell sizes are small; in that case, they are based on the Fisher exact test.

[c] The number of countries changes over the duration of the panel.

[d] Percent of country years in which nations experienced high levels of political turmoil—riots, demonstrations, protests, strikes, etc.—as recorded by Arthur Banks in his Cross National Time Series Archive, www.databanksinternational.com/53.html. By "high" I mean above the median value.

[e] Percent of country years in which presidents or prime ministers made "irregular exits" from office, as reported in the Archigos data set compiled by Hein Goemans, www.rochester.edu/college/faculty/hgoemans/data.html.

[f] Relative frequency of civil wars, as recorded in the Armed Conflict Data Set compiled by the Peace Research Institute of Oslo and the Uppsala Conflict Data Program, www.nsdnuib.ho/macrodataguide. The definition of a civil war is contained in this source; I use a 100 battle deaths as my cut-off point. The differences reported in this column are robust to the choice of cut-point.

[g] The data on state failure come from Polity IV. When researchers at Polity could find no evidence of a government, they judged the country to have fallen into anarchy and coded the case −77. See the Polity IV User's Manual, www.systemic.peace\insca\p4manualv2012.pdf. Countries so classified were judged failed states.

As shown in table A.2, not only are countries in the developing world more likely to suffer political instability; they are also more likely to suffer economic reversals. While the presence of regional inequality is unrelated to the incidence of growth reversals, countries with high levels of ethnic polarization, diversity, or indirect rule exhibit significantly greater levels of economic volatility.[7]

Table A.3 demonstrates that where there is political conflict, growth reversals are more likely. State failure lowers the growth rate by a full nine percentage points; "irregular" exits reduce it by over three. Riots and demonstrations have a smaller but still significant impact on growth. In some cases—and especially in the case of state failure—the impact is long-lasting. In the case of state failure, for example, data not shown here suggest that even after five years, the rate of growth fails to recover to its previous level.[8] The growth trajectories traced by developing countries are thus significantly related to their politics.[9]

In table A.4, we move from bivariate to multivariate analysis. In these estimates, the growth rate of per capita income is the dependent variable; as is standard, we control for the initial level of GDP per capita. In each equation, a different measure of political disorder is included. Standard errors are clustered by country and fixed effects entered for both country and period. Comparing the results in this table with those above (table A.2), we note that when indicators of political violence are included in the equations, the coefficients for variables that characterize the political terrain become insignificant.[10] That this is the case suggests that the impact of the political terrain is in effect impounded into the nation's politics.

TABLE A.2. Economic Volatility (GDP drops, 1970–2012)

	Number of Country Years[d]	Negative Growth	Negative Growth or 3% + Drop	Negative Growth or 4% + Drop	Negative Growth or 5% + Drop	Negative Growth or 6% + Drop
Colonies[a]	4,313	30.88%	38.12%	35.45%	33.78%	32.85%
Non-Colonies	2,381	22.68%	28.98%	26.59%	24.78%	23.73%
Pearson's Chi		37.04	38.59	38.60	42.11	44.78
p value		0.00	0.00	0.00	0.00	0.00
Regional Inequality = Yes	3,479	28.05%	34.46%	32.05%	30.30%	29.35%
Regional Inequality = No	3,215	27.87%	35.30%	32.57%	30.89%	29.89%
Pearson's Chi		0.65	0.00	0.07	0.03	0.04
p-value		0.42	0.96	0.79	0.87	0.85
High Ethnic Polarization[b]	3,072	30.334%	37.08%	34.83%	33.27%	32.29%
Low Ethnic Polarization	2,113	24.94%	31.28%	28.63%	26.88%	26.08%
Pearson's Chi		17.62	17.95	21.36	23.37	23.37
p-value		0.00	0.00	0.00	0.00	0.00
High Indirect Rule[c]	2,696	32.64%	38.95%	36.57%	35.31%	34.42%
Low Indirect Rule	972	25.41%	31.48%	28.70%	27.26%	26.13%

Pearson's Chi	6.0066	4.49	6.36	7.42	8.65	
p-value	0.014	0.03	0.01	0.01	0.00	
High ELF Score	2,419	30.96%	37.41%	35.18%	33.86%	32.70%
Low ELF Score	3,082	24.95%	31.34%	28.55%	26.90%	26.12%
Pearson's Chi	36.4516	35.48	41.28	45.20	41.62	
p-value	0.00	0.00	0.00	0.00	0.00	

Note: Significance levels are based on the chi-square statistic, save when cell sizes are small; in that case, they are based on the Fisher exact test. Data on regional inequality were gathered from data compiled by William Nordhaus and his colleagues (http://gecon.yale.edu) from photographs of the earth taken at night by satellites that record the intensity of artificial light. The intensity of the illumination, they contend, provides a measure of urbanization and energy use, and thus the extent of economic development. Countries judged by a panel of undergraduate researchers as exhibiting pronounced regional differences in the intensity of "night lights" were classified in the first group (labeled "Yes"); others were placed in the second. The ethnic polarization variable is based on the configuration of the size distribution of subnational groups and has repeatedly been found to be significantly related to political conflict. J. G. Montalvo and M. Reynal-Querol, "Ethnic Polarization, Potential Conflict, and Civil Wars," *American Economic Review* 95, no. 3 (2005): 796–816 find that the higher the value of the measure, the greater the likelihood of conflict. Data on economic growth came from the World Bank's World Development Indicators, http://data.worldbank.org/data-catalog/world-development-indicators. Ethnic fractionalization is a measure of diversity. It is calculated as the probability, if drawn by random from a nation's population, two persons will come from different ethnolinguistic groups.

[a] Countries that were colonies at any time between 1800 and 2000, excluding Australia, Canada, and New Zealand.

[b] The measures of polarization, fractionalization, and indirect rule: Countries in which these characteristics assume values lying above the median are classified "high" while those in which these characteristics assume values lying below the median are classified as "low." Countries with the measure of ethnic polarization > +0.5 are rated high. So too are those whose measure of indirect rule is >=0.

[c] Indirect rule is a measure based upon the ratio of court cases heard in "traditional courts" divided by the total number of cases. Based on data originally collected by M. Lange, "British Colonial State Legacies and Development Trajectories: A Statistical Analysis of Direct and Indirect Rule," in *States and Development: Historical Antecedents of Stagnation and Advance,* ed. M. Lange and D. Rueschemeyer (New York: Palgrave Macmillan, 2005), 117–39. Hariri imputes the values for other developing nations, as reported in J. G. Hariri, "The Autocratic Legacy of Early Statehood," *American Political Science Review* 106, no. 3 (2012): 471–94.

[d] The number of countries changes over the duration of the panel.

TABLE A.3. Political Instability and Economic Volatility

| Dependent Variable: Annual Rate of Growth of Per Capita GDP[a] | | | | |
Independent Variable	Riots and Demonstrations[b]	Irregular Political Exit[c]	Civil War[d]	State Failure[e]
Coefficient	−0.124	−3.397	−1.081	−9.033
Standard Error	(0.034)	(0.384)	(0.277)	(0.612)
Significance Level	0.0	0.0	0.0	0.0

Note: To prevent bias arising from the impact of growth on violence, these coefficients were computed using the generalized method of moments estimator of Arellano and Bond.

[a] The data on the annual growth rates came from the World Bank's World Development Indicators, http://data.worldbank.org/data-catalog/world-development-indicators.

[b] Percent of country years in which nations experienced high levels of political turmoil—riots, demonstrations, protests, strikes, etc.—as reported by Arthur Banks in his Cross National Time Series Archive, www.databanksinternational.com/53.html. By "high" I mean above the median value.

[c] Percent of country years in which presidents or prime ministers made "irregular exits" from office, as reported in the Archigos data set compiled by Hein Goemans, www.rochester.edu/college/faculty/hgoemans/data,html.

[d] Relative frequency of civil wars, as recorded in the Armed Conflict Data Set compiled by the Peace Research Institute of Oslo and the Uppsala Conflict Data Program, www.nsdnuib.ho/macrodataguide. The definition of a civil war is contained in this source; I use a 100 battle deaths as my cut-off point. The differences reported in this column are robust to the choice of cut-point.

[e] The data on state failure come from Polity IV. When researchers at Polity could find no evidence of a government, they judged the country to have fallen into anarchy and coded the case −77. We took that as indicating state failure. See the Polity IV User's Manual, www.systemic,peace\insca\p4manualv2012.pdf.

TABLE A.4. Regression Analysis (Arellano and Bond GMM estimator)

| | Dependent Variable: Annual Rate of Growth of Per Capita GDP[d] | | | |
| | Independent Variables | | | |
Independent Variables	Riots and Demonstrations[e]	Irregular Exits from Power[f]	Civil War[g]	State Failure[b]
Independent Variables	-0.00213***	-0.0416***	-0.0149***	-0.0917***
	(0.000808)	(0.00895)	(0.00714)	(0.0298)
Ethnic Polarization[a]	0.196	-0.0473	0.0816	-0.108
	(0.0707)	(0.0362)	(0.0704)	(0.0972)
Regional Inequality[b]	0.0718*	0.0143	0.00223	0.0242**
	(0.0383)	(0.0220)	(0.0233)	(0.00960)
Indirect Rule[c]	-0.0281	0.0173	-0.0119	-0.00425
	(0.0285)	(0.0384)	(0.0141)	(0.00998)
Initial GDP[d]	0.00000151	0.00000117	0.00000129*	0.000000737
	(0.00000132)	(0.00000114)	(0.000000712)	(0.000000723)
Constant	0.0158	0.0657*	-0.00307	0.110*
	(0.0572)	(0.0395)	(0.0461)	(0.0602)
Period Dummies	YES	YES	YES	YES
Country Fixed Effects	YES	YES	YES	YES

(continued)

TABLE A.4. (*continued*)

| | Independent Variables | | | |
	Riots and Demonstrations[e]	Irregular Exits from Power[f]	Civil War[g]	State Failure[h]
Observations	3,370	3,357	3,620	3,815
Number of Countries	81	82	91	81

Note: Standard errors clustered by country.

[a] The ethnic polarization variable is based on the configuration of the size distribution of subnational groups. The more a nation's population is gathered into a bipolar and symmetrical distribution of ethnic groups, the higher the level of polarization. See J. G. Montalvo and M. Reynal-Querol, "Ethnic Polarization, Potential Conflict, and Civil Wars," *American Economic Review* 95, no. 3 (2005): 796–816.

[b] Data on regional inequality were gathered from data compiled by William Nordhaus and his colleagues (http://gecon.yale.edu) from photographs of the earth taken at night by satellites that record the intensity of artificial light. The intensity of the illumination, they contend, provides a measure of urbanization and energy use, and thus the extent of economic development. Countries judged by a panel of undergraduate researchers as exhibiting pronounced regional differences in the intensity of "night lights" were classified "Yes."

[c] Indirect rule is a measure based upon the ratio of court cases heard in "traditional courts" divided by the total number of cases. Based on data originally collected by M. Lange. "British Colonial State Legacies and Development Trajectories: A Statistical Analysis of Direct and Indirect Rule," in *States and Development: Historical Antecedents of Stagnation and Advance*, ed. M. Lange and D. Rueschemeyer (New York: Palgrave Macmillan, 2005), 117–39. Hariri imputed the values for other developing nations, as reported in J. G. Hariri, "The Autocratic Legacy of Early Statehood," *American Political Science Review* 106, no. 3 (2012): 471–94.

[d] Data from the World Bank's World Development Indicators, http://data.worldbank.org/data-catalog/world-development-indicators.

[e] Percent of country years in which nations experienced high levels of political turmoil—riots, demonstrations, protests, strikes, etc.—as recorded by Arthur Banks in his Cross National Time Series Archive, www.databanksinternational.com/53.html. By "high" I mean above the median value.

[f] Percent of country years in which presidents or prime ministers made "irregular exits" from office, as reported in the Archigos data set compiled by Hein Goemans, www.rochester.edu/college/faculty/hgoemans/data.html.

[g] Relative frequency of civil wars, as recorded in the Armed Conflict Data Set compiled by the Peace Research Institute of Oslo and the Uppsala Conflict Data Program, www.nsd.uib.no/macrodataguide. This source contains the definition of a civil war employed; I use a 100 battle deaths as my cut-off point. The differences reported in this column are robust to the choice of cut-point.

[h] The data on state failure come from Polity IV. When researchers at Polity could find no evidence of a government, they judged the country to have fallen into anarchy and coded the case −77. Polity IV User's Manual, www.systemic.peace\insca\p4manualv2012.pdf.

*p < .10
**p < .05
***p < .01

NOTES

Preface

1. R. H. Bates, *Analytic Narratives* (Princeton: Princeton University Press, 1998).

Chapter 1: Introduction

1. R. E. Lucas, "On the Mechanics of Economic Development," *Journal of Monetary Economics* 22 (1998): 3–42, 5.

2. T. Hobbes, *Leviathan*, Great Political Thinkers, ed. W. Ebenstein (New York: Holt, Reinhart and Winston, 1961), 368.

3. D. Ricardo, *On the Principles of Political Economy and Taxation* (London: John Murray, 1817). A key assumption underlying this argument is the absence of technical change, something challenged by Boserup, among others. E. Boserup, *The Conditions of Agricultural Growth* (London: G. Allen and Unwin, 1965).

4. See the discussion in C. P. Timmer and W. P. Falcon, *Food Policy Analysis* (Baltimore: Johns Hopkins University Press for the World Bank, 1983); D. Perkins, S. C. Radelet, et al., *Economics of Development* (New York: W. W. Norton, 2012).

5. Assuming that a small portion of the annual food crop is externally traded, an assumption that finds support in the literature.

6. S. Kuznets, *Modern Economic Growth* (New Haven: Yale University Press, 1966); H. B. Chenery and L. Taylor, "Development Patterns: Among Countries and over Time," *Review of Economics and Statistics* 50, no. 4 (November 1968): 391–416.

7. Most notably, by K. Polanyi, *The Great Transformation* (Boston: Beacon Press, 1944).

8. See, for example, M. Gluckman, *Custom and Conflict in Africa* (Oxford: Blackwell, 1955); M. Sahlins, "Tribal Economies," in *Economic Development and Social Change*, ed. G. Dalton (Garden City, NY: Natural History Press for the American Museum of Natural History, 1971), 43–61; E. Colson, *Tradition and Contract: The Problem of Order* (Chicago: Aldine, 1974).

9. For an illuminating discussion of the impact of these regions on Europe, see J. L. Abu-Lughod, *Before European Hegemony: The World System, 1250–1350* (Oxford: Oxford University Press, 1989) and the discussion of K. O. Kupperman, ed., *America in European Consciousness, 1493–1750* (Chapel Hill: University of North Carolina Press for the Institute of Early American History and Culture, 1995).

The transition from a Ricardian world is often first marked by the rise of the textile industry. When Europe started producing cotton textiles in the sixteenth century, it was unable to compete with China and India, both of which were able to ship finished cotton cloth to Europe at a price below the local costs of production. As Beckert states, "Europe's first incursion into the world of cotton collapsed in the face of superior power." S. Beckert, *Empire of Cotton* (New York: Alfred A. Knopf, 2014), 30.

10. For clarification, consult the chapters ahead and the addendum to this chapter.

11. B. Weingast, "The Economic Role of Political Institutions," *Journal of Law, Economics, and Organization* 7, no. 1 (1995): 1–31, quote on 1.

12. S. P. Huntington, *Political Order in Changing Societies* (New Haven: Yale University Press, 1968).

13. D. Acemoglu and J. A. Robinson, *Why Nations Fail: The Origins of Power, Prosperity, and Poverty* (New York: Crown, 2012).

14. D. C. North, J. J. Wallis, et al., *Violence and Social Orders* (New York: Cambridge University Press, 2009).

15. R. Brenner, "Agrarian Class Structure and Economic Development in Pre-Industrial Europe," *Past and Present* 70 (February 1976): 30–75.

16. R. Emerson, *From Empire to Nation* (Boston: Beacon Press, 1962); D. Apter, ed., *Old Societies and New States* (New York: Free Press of Glencoe, 1963); C. Geertz, "The Integrative Revolution: Primordial Sentiments and Civil Politics in the New States," in *Old Societies and New States*, ed. Apter; R. L. Sklar, *Nigerian Political Parties* (Princeton: Princeton University Press, 1963); J. S. Coleman and C. G. Rosberg, *Political Parties and National Integration* (Berkeley: University of California Press, 1964); C. W. Anderson, F. R. von der Mehden, et al., *Issues of Political Development* (Englewood Cliffs, NJ: Prentice-Hall, 1967); R. L. Sklar, "Political Science and National Integration: A Radical Approach," *Journal of Modern African Studies* 5 (May 1967): 1–11; M. Weiner, *Sons of the Soil: Migration and Ethnic Conflict in India* (Princeton: Princeton University Press, 1978).

Chapter 2: The Fundamental Tension

1. See the addendum to this chapter. See as well R. H. Bates, A. Greif, et al., "Organizing Violence," *Journal of Conflict Resolution* 46, no. 5 (October 2002): 599–628.

2. G. Wolf, *Becoming Roman: The Origins of Provincial Civilization* (New York: Cambridge University Press, 1998); J.-P. Devroey, "The Economy," in *The Early Middle Ages: Europe, 400–1000*, ed. R. McKitterick (Oxford: Oxford University Press, 2003), 97–130.

3. M. McCormick, *Origins of the European Economy* (New York: Cambridge University Press, 2005), 29.

4. Devroey, "The Economy"; McCormick, *Origins of the European Economy*.

5. G. Ausenda, ed., *After Empire: Towards an Ethnology of Europe's Barbarians*, Studies in Historical Archaeoethnology (Woodbridge: Boydell Press, 1995); G. Hal-

sall, *Barbarian Migrations and the Roman West, 376–568* (Cambridge: Cambridge University Press, 2007).

6. R. H. S. Van Bath, *The Agrarian History of Western Europe, 500–1850* (London: Edward Arnold, 1963); M. Bloch, *Feudal Society* (Chicago: University of Chicago Press, 1970); F. Lotter, "The Crusading Idea and the Conquest of the Region East of the Elbe," in *Medieval Frontier Societies*, ed. R. Bartlett (Oxford: Clarendon, 1989), 267–306.

7. Van Bath, *The Agrarian History of Western Europe.*

8. D. Whittaker and J. Goody, "Rural Manufacturing in the Rouergue from Antiquity to the Present: The Examples of Pottery and Cheese," *Comparative Studies in Society and History* 43, no. 2 (2001): 225–45, quotes on 243.

9. D. C. Coleman, "Proto-Industrialization: A Concept Too Many," *Economic History Review* 36, no. 3 (1983): 435–88.

10. W. N. Parker and E. L. Jones, eds., *European Peasants and Their Markets* (Princeton: Princeton University Press, 1975).

11. For overviews, see R. Lopez, *The Commercial Revolution of the Middle Ages, 939–1350* (New York: Cambridge University Press, 1976) and S. A. Epstein, *An Economic and Social History of Later Medieval Europe, 1000–1500* (New York: Cambridge University Press, 2009).

12. See Abu-Lughod, *Before European Hegemony*; R. Finlay and K. H. O'Rourke, *Power and Plenty: Trade, War and the World Economy in the Second Millennium* (Princeton: Princeton University Press, 2009).

13. F. C. Lane, *Venice and History: The Collected Papers of Frederic C. Lane* (Baltimore: Johns Hopkins University Press, 1966).

14. J. Edwards and S. Ogilvie, "What Lessons for Economic Development Can We Draw from the Champagne Fairs?" *Journal of Economic History* 49 (2012): 131–48.

15. G. Duby, *France in the Middle Ages, 987–1460* (Oxford: Blackwell, 1987), 155.

16. G. Duby, *Medieval Marriage: Two Models from Twelfth-Century France* (Baltimore: Johns Hopkins University Press, 1978); G. Duby, *The Knight, the Lady, and the Priest: The Making of Modern Marriage in Medieval France* (Chicago: University of Chicago Press, 1981); J. Goody, *The Development of the Family and Marriage in Europe* (Cambridge: Cambridge University Press, 1983); H. J. Berman, *Law and Revolution: The Formation of the Western Legal Tradition* (Cambridge, MA: Harvard University Press, 1988); T. N. Bisson, *The Crisis of the Twelfth Century* (Princeton: Princeton University Press, 2009).

17. See T. Head and R. Landes, eds., *The Peace of God* (Ithaca: Cornell University Press, 1992). See also the discussion in Berman, *Law and Revolution.*

18. Including by taking their violent conduct elsewhere. Thus Urban II's speech to the Council of Clermont 1095, in which he advocated the launching of the first crusade: "Let those who have been accustomed unjustly to wage private warfare against the faithful now go against the infidels and end with victory this war which should have been begun long ago. Let those who for a long time, have been robbers, now

become knights. Let those who have been fighting against their brothers and relatives now fight in a proper way against the barbarians. Let those who have been serving as mercenaries for small pay now obtain the eternal reward. [L]et them eagerly set out on the way with God as their guide." From Bongars, *Gesta Dei per Francos*, 1, pp. 382 ff., trans. in Oliver J. Thatcher and Edgar Holmes McNeal, eds., *A Source Book for Medieval History* (New York: Scribner's, 1905), 513–17. See http://www.fordham .edu/halsall/source/urban2-fulcher.html.

19. The Church also founded military orders to enforce these codes. While these units joined in the crusades and fought largely outside of Europe, some remained and others returned, thus seeding Europe with living examples of "Christian virtue" in arms.

20. M. Keen, *Chivalry* (New Haven: Yale University Press, 1984).

21. He appears to have been a remarkably effective administrator and planted the seeds of the long-term transition from familial to bureaucratic power in France. Duby, *France in the Middle Ages*.

22. Berman, *Law and Revolution*; Bisson, *The Crisis of the Twelfth Century*. Both scholars note that the peace movements resulted in the production of law. Some of the laws appear trivial, such as those that banned fighting on particular days. But others, they note, took the form of comprehensive acts that defined what constituted actionable instances of disorder and that enumerated the sanctions and remedies to be applied.

23. Most notably, Henry, Bishop of Winchester, who exercised great power—and accumulated extraordinary wealth—while in the service of Henry I.

24. R. H. C. Davis, "What Happened in Stephen's Reign, 1135–1154," *History* 49, no. 165 (1964): 1–12; J. T. Appleby, *The Troubled Reign of King Stephen* (London: G. Bell and Sons, 1969); R. H. C. Davis, *King Stephen, 1135–1154* (London: Longman, 1990); E. King, ed., *The Anarchy of King Stephen's Reign* (Oxford: Clarendon, 1994); J. Bradbury, *Stephen and Matilda: The Civil War of 1139–53* (Summerset, Fromme: Alan Sutton Publishing, 1996).

25. King, *The Anarchy of King Stephen's Reign*, 135.

26. A. R. Hogue, *The Origins of Common Law* (Bloomington: Indiana University Press, 1966); J. Hudson, *The Formation of the English Common Law* (New York: Longman, 1996).

27. I am drawing here from Bates, Greif, et al., "Organizing Violence." See also J. D. Fearon and D. D. Latin, "Explaining Interethnic Cooperation," *American Political Science Review* 90 (December 1996): 715–35; M. J. L. Hardy, *Blood Feuds and the Payment of Blood Money in the Middle East* (Beirut: Catholic Press, 1963); C. Boehm, *Blood Revenge* (Philadelphia: University of Pennsylvania Press, 1984); and R. Fletcher, *Blood Feud* (Oxford: Oxford University Press, 2003). See also D. S. Allen, *The World of Prometheus: The Politics of Punishing in Democratic Athens* (Princeton: Princeton University Press, 2002).

28. C. Tilly, "War Making and State Making as Organized Crime," in *Bringing the State Back In*, ed. P. Evans, D. Rueschemeyer, and T. Skocpol (Cambridge: Cambridge University Press, 1985); C. Tilly, *Coercion, Capital and European States, AD 900–1990* (Oxford: Oxford University Press, 1990).

29. To borrow the phrases of Islam, states are characterized by two zones: one in which disputes can be settled peacefully—the Dar al-Salaam—and zones where they give way to war—the Dar al-Harb. Tilly focuses on the latter; but in Europe, the Dar al-Salaam came first.

Chapter 3: Taming the Hierarchy?

1. Recall that the invasion of England was the second major exodus from Normandy, the conquest of Sicily being the first. The accounts of the Normans' preparations for the invasion of England largely come from E. Searle, *Predatory Kinship and the Creation of Norman Power, 840–1066* (Berkeley: University of California Press, 1988).

2. In a typical fashion, they mixed avarice with fealty. In an effort to attract stakeholders, they presented their plans and prospectus at public meetings, offering to share the proceeds in exchange for military backing.

3. Searle, *Predatory Kinship and the Creation of Norman Power*.

4. G. Barraclough, *The Crucible of Europe: The Ninth and Tenth Centuries in European History* (Berkeley: University of Californa Press, 1976); see also J. F. Benton, ed., *Town Origins: The Evidence from Medieval England* (Lexington, MA: D. C. Heath, 1968). As stated by Stenton: so great was the purge that "English names fell from the rolls of the shires, to be replaced by the names of Normans." F. M. Stenton, "Presidential Address: English Families and the Norman Conquest," *Transactions of the Royal Historical Society* 26 (1944): 1–12, quote on 8.

5. Stenton, "Presidential Address: English Families and the Norman Conquest," 8.

6. Thus laying the foundation for one of the world's most unequal distributions of property.

7. See M. Weber, *Basic Concepts in Sociology* (Seacaucus, NJ: Citadel, 1985).

8. E. Weber, *Peasants into Frenchmen* (Stanford: Stanford University Press, 1976).

9. F. F. Mendels, "Proto-Industrialization: The First Phase of the Industrialization Process," *Journal of Economic History* 32, no. 1 (1972): 241–61; J. De Vries, *European Urbanization, 1500–1800* (Cambridge, MA: Harvard University Press, 1984); Coleman, "Proto-Industrialization."

10. J. W. Baldwin, *The Government of Philip Augustus* (Berkeley: University of California Press, 1986).

11. The great exception was Provence, where a mixture of religious and dynastic motives led to a fierce harrowing of the region.

12. See D. Jones, *The Wars of the Roses* (New York: Penguin, 2014), map 3.

13. Consider too the Yorks themselves: while their land clustered in a culturally distinctive region—that of Wales—when they fought, it was to seize control of the central hierarchy.

14. Had Marshall Sahlins explored the lineage's behavior, he would have noted the same "predatory" character that he associated with lineages in Africa. M. D. Sahlins,

"The Segmentary Lineage: An Organization of Predatory Expansion," *American Anthropologist* 63 (1961): 322–45.

15. Duby, *France in the Middle Ages*, 286.

16. E. Power, *The Wool Trade in English Medieval History* (Oxford: Oxford University Press, 1941), 13.

17. For a superb account of Flanders in this period, see D. Boulger, *The History of Belgium: Part I—Caesar to Waterloo* (Laurel, MD: Elibron Classics, 2005).

18. Many consider these consultations to be the origins of Parliament.

19. It appears that those administering the monopoly found ways of consuming the rents it generated. Certainly, its members were often charged with corruption and not infrequently convicted.

20. The discussion here is drawn from: A. F. Pollard, *The Evolution of Parliament* (London: Longman, 1926); J. F. Willard, *Parliamentary Taxation of Personal Property, 1290 to 1334* (Cambridge, MA: Medieval Academy of America, 1934); G. L. Harris, *King, Parliament, and Public Finance in Medieval England to 1369* (Oxford: Clarendon, 1975); J. O. Prestwich, "War and Finance in the Anglo-Norman State," *Transactions of the Royal Historical Society*, 5th ser., 4 (1954): 19–54; M. Prestwich, *War, Politics and Finance under Edward I* (London: Faber and Faber, 1972); G. Holmes, *The Good Parliament* (Oxford: Clarendon, 1975); and J. H. Munro, "The Symbiosis of Towns and Textiles: Urban Institutions and the Changing Fortunes of Cloth Manufacturing in the Low Countries and England, 1270–1570" (MPRA Paper No. 11266, Department of Economics, University of Toronto, 1998); see also M. Levi, *Of Rule and Revenue* (Berkeley: University of California Press, 1988). It should be noted that while public revenues financed much of the costs of war, so too did plunder. Many of the troops had been raised by grandees who sought to add to their estates by pillaging the French countryside. The booty thus seized financed the building of some of the "great houses" that ornament the English countryside.

21. While not wanting to endorse Fontescue's idealization of the English system, his account does capture an important point: the aristocracy in England played a far greater role in national and local politics than it did in France. I discuss this point further later in the chapter. S. J. Fontescue, *The Governance of England* (Oxford: Oxford University Press, 1885).

22. Note that this discussion provides a political account of the origins of private property. They lie as much in the politics of the legislature as they do in rulings by the courts.

23. Note Hintze's characterization of the behavior of institutions that represent classes—my word, not his—as opposed to geographic districts. F. Gilbert and R. M. Berdhal, eds., *The Historical Essays of Otto Hintze* (New York: Oxford University Press, 1975).

24. S. L. Kaplan, *Bread, Politics and Political Economy in the Reign of Louis XV* (The Hague: Martinus Nijhoff, 1976); S. L. Kaplan, *Provisioning Paris: Merchants and Millers in the Grain and Flour Trade during the Eighteenth Century*, 2 vols. (Ithaca: Cornell University Press, 1984).

25. A. Smith, *An Inquiry into the Nature and Causes of the Wealth of Nations*, ed. E. Cannan (Chicago: University of Chicago Press, 1976), book 4, chapter 5.

26. R. Brenner, *Merchants and Revolution: Commercial Change, Political Conflict, and London's Overseas Traders, 1550–1653* (Princeton: Princeton University Press, 1993), 89.

27. The phrase comes from M. Lipton, *Urban Bias* (London: Temple Smith, 1977).

28. R. C. Allen, "The Nitrogen Hypothesis and the English Agricultural Revolution: A Biological Analysis," *Journal of Economic History* 68 (2008): 182–210. See also P. Timmer, "The Turnip, the New Husbandry, and the English Agricultural Revolution," *Quarterly Journal of Economics* 83, no. 3 (1969): 375–95.

29. Because food is a necessity, as prices change, the amount consumed fails to change in proportion.

30. As stressed by Allen, urban consumers in England enjoyed better diets than did those in France, even though spending a lower percentage of their incomes on food. See R. O. Allen, *The British Industrial Revolution in Global Perspective* (New York: Cambridge University Press, 2009); R. H. Bates, "Lessons from History, or the Perfidy of English Exceptionalism and the Significance of Historical France," *World Politics* 40, no. 4 (1988): 499–516; P. Lindert, "Historical Patterns of Agricultural Policy," in *Agriculture and the State*, ed. P. Timmer (Ithaca: Cornell University Press, 1991), 29–83.

31. P. Hoffman, *Growth in a Traditional Society: The French Countryside, 1450–1815* (Princeton: Princeton University Press, 1996).

32. Similar procedures were used to determine rights-of-way for new roads and "turnpikes," i.e., toll roads built by private companies. See D. Bogart, "Turnpike Trusts and the Transportation Revolution in Eighteenth Century England," *Explorations in Economic History* 65 (2005): 439–68; D. Bogart, "Turnpike Trusts and Property Income," *Economic History Review* 62, no. 1 (2009): 128–52.

33. And thus their ability to pay taxes. See A. de Tocqueville, *The Ancien Regime and the Revolution*, trans. Stuart Gilbert (London: Penguin, 2008).

34. P. Hoffman, "Institutions and Agriculture in Old Regime France," *Politics and Society* 16, no. 2–3 (1988): 241–64; J.-L. Rosenthal, *The Fruits of Revolution: Property Rights, Litigation, and French Agriculture, 1700–1860* (New York: Cambridge University Press, 1992); Hoffman, *Growth in a Traditional Society*.

35. J. Brewer, *The Sinews of Power: War, Money and the English State, 1688–1783* (New York: Knopf, 1988).

36. Smith, *An Inquiry into the Nature and Causes of the Wealth of Nations*, book 1, page 219.

37. W. Beik, *Absolutism and Society in Seventeenth-Century France: State Power and Provincial Aristocracy in Languedoc* (New York: Cambridge University Press, 1989). The *fouage*, for example, was a tax on urban real estate and numbered among the most lucrative of the monarch's levies, but the regional assembly in Languedoc deemed the tax a violation of ancient customs. J. B. Henneman, "Nobility, Privilege

and Fiscal Politics in Late Medieval France," *French Historical Studies* 13, no. 1 (1983): 1–17. In the end, Languedoc did pay.

38. Contrast the inefficiency of the French system with the performance of that in England, as documented in Brewer, *The Sinews of Power*. For an analysis of the performance of the regionalized as opposed to centralized tax system in Europe, see M. Dincecco, *Political Transformation and Public Finances, Europe: 1650–1913* (New York: Cambridge University Press, 2011).

39. D. Bien, "Les offices, les corps et le credit d'état," *Annales* 43 (1988): 379–404. For a discussion of a third source of loans, *rentes* or annuities, see P. Hoffman, G. Postel-Vinay, et al., *Priceless Markets: The Political Economy of Credit in Paris, 1660–1870* (Chicago: University of Chicago Press, 2000).

40. Hoffman, Postel-Vinay, et al., *Priceless Markets*, 21.

41. C. Bastable, *Public Finance* (London: Macmillan, 1917), chapter 4, para. 1, "The Online Library of Liberty," http://oll.libertyfund.org. See also T. J. Sargent and F. O. R. Velde, "Macroeconomic Features of the French Revolution," *Journal of Political Economy* 103, no. 3 (1995): 474–518.

42. In the eighteenth century alone, the monarch "restructured" his finances five times. Bastable, *Public Finance*, 254. See also D. Dessert and J.-L. Journet, "Le Lobby Colbert: Un Royaume, ou un affaire de famille?" *Annales* 30, no. 6 (1975): 1303–36.

43. F. R. Velde and D. R. Weir, "The Financial Market and Government Debt Policy in France, 1746–1793," *Journal of Economic History* 52, no. 1 (1992): 1–39

Chapter 4: Forging the Political Terrain.

1. I wish to acknowledge my debt to Kathryn Firmin-Sellers and Jeffrey Herbst, whose writings anticipate the arguments of this chapter. See K. Firmin-Sellers, *The Transformation of Property Rights in the Gold Coast: An Empirical Study Applying Rational Choice Theory*, Political Economy of Institutions and Decisions (Cambridge: Cambridge University Press, 1996) and J. Herbst, *States and Power in Africa* (Princeton: Princeton University Press, 2000).

2. Using the Google tool Ngrams.

3. Other phrases were tried and appeared with much the same frequency.

4. The classic treatments remain Tilly, *Coercion, Capital and European States*; M. Roberts, *The Military Revolution, 1560–1660* (Belfast: M. Boyd, 1956); G. Parker, *The Military Revolution: Military Innovation and the Rise of the West, 1500–1800* (New York: Cambridge University Press, 1991); B. M. Downing, *The Military Revolution and Political Change* (Princeton: Princeton University Press, 1992).

5. S. Pincus and J. A. Robinson, "The Glorious Revolution Revisited," in *The New Institutional History: Essays in Honor of Douglass North*, ed. I. Sened (New York: Cambridge University Press, 2013), 198.

6. The population data come from A. Maddison, *The World Economy* (Paris: Organization for Economic Cooperation & Development, 2006).

7. *The Economist*, July 13, 2013, p. 5. For thoughtful discussion of the Sykes-Picot Agreement, see E. Rogan, *The Fall of the Ottomans* (New York: Basic Books, 2015), 285ff., 357ff.

8. Jeffrey Herbst gives an excellent treatment of the conference. See his *States and Power in Africa*.

9. P. Brendon, *The Decline and Fall of the British Empire, 1781–1997* (New York: Vintage, 2007), 98.

10. E. Huillery, "The Black Man's Burden: The Cost of Colonization of French West Africa," *Journal of Economic History* 74, no. 1 (2014): 1–38; E. Huillery, *French West Africa: Did Prosperous Areas Fall Behind?* (Paris: Paris School of Economics, 2008).

11. A. Alesina and E. Spolare, *The Size of Nations* (Cambridge, MA: MIT Press, 2003).

12. Fearon and Laitin, "Explaining Interethnic Cooperation."

13. For a persuasive debunking of its distinctively British character, see C. Boone, *Political Topographies of the African State: Rural Authority and Institutional Choice* (Cambridge: Cambridge University Press, 2003).

14. C. K. Meek, *Land Law and Custom in the Colonies* (London: Oxford University Press, 1949), 10.

15. R. H. Bates, *Unions, Parties, and Political Development* (New Haven: Yale University Press, 1971); R. H. Bates, *Rural Responses to Industrialization* (New Haven: Yale University Press, 1976); R. H. Bates, *Beyond the Miracle of the Market* (Cambridge: Cambridge University Press, 1989).

16. More accurately, the data were assembled by Kaiyang Huang, Ahsan Barkatullah, and Didi Kuo and her intrepid undergraduate assistants, whose names appear in the preface.

17. Thus placing Latin America among the "Post-Colonial" nations. Being settler nations, Canada, New Zealand, and Australia are not classified as former colonies.

18. The data were downloaded from the website of James Fearon, https://web .stanford.edu/group/fearon-research/cgi-bin/wordpress/.

19. See J. G. Montalvo and M. Reynal-Querol, "Ethnic Polarization, Potential Conflict, and Civil Wars," *American Economic Review* 95, no. 3 (2005): 796–816; J. G. Montalvo and M. Reynal-Querol, "Discrete Polarization with an Application to the Determinants of Genocide," *Economic Journal* 118 (November 2008): 1835–65.

20. The data can be found at http://gecon.yale.edu.

21. As judged by the Fisher exact test.

22. J. G. Hariri, "The Autocratic Legacy of Early Statehood," *American Political Science Review* 106, no. 3 (2012): 471–94, 473n7.

23. As Hariri notes, the measure was devised by Matthew Lange: M. Lange, "British Colonial Legacies and Political Development," *World Development* 32, no. 6 (2004): 905–22; M. Lange, "British Colonial State Legacies and Development Trajectories: A Statistical Analysis of Direct and Indirect Rule," in *States and Development: Historical Antecedents of Stagnation and Advance*, ed. M. Lange and D. Rueschemeyer

(New York: Palgrave Macmillan, 2005), 117–39. The settler data are taken from D. Acemoglu, J. A. Robsinson, et al., "The Colonial Origins of Comparative Development," *American Economic Review* 91, no. 5 (2001): 1369–1401.

24. He did so by calculating the relationship between the number of European settlers and Lange's measure of indirect rule. Where the data on settlers are available and Lange's index not—e.g., in French or Portuguese colonies—the relationship is then used to impute the value of the latter.

Chapter 5: The Developing World

1. Known as Northern Rhodesia before becoming independent in 1964.

2. For an excellent essay on the Congress of Berlin, see Herbst, *States and Power in Africa*. Turn as well to T. Pakenham, *The Scramble for Africa: 1876–1912* (London: Weidenfeld and Nicolson, 1991); M. Meredith, *The Fortunes of Africa: A 5000-Year History of Wealth, Greed, and Endeavor* (New York: Public Affairs, 2014).

3. J. M. Davis, *Modern Industry and the African* (London: Macmillan, 1933); W. J. Barber, *The Economy of British Central Africa* (London: Oxford University Press, 1961); L. H. Gann, *A History of Northern Rhodesia: Early Days to 1953* (London: Chatto and Windus, 1964); R. E. Baldwin, *Economic Development and Export Growth: A Study of Northern Rhodesia, 1920–1960* (Berkeley: University of California Press, 1966).

4. Some, such as the Ila and Tonga, lacked any political hierarchy; they were societies without states. Others, such as the Lozi, Bemba, and Lunda, possess centralized polities. See M. Fortes and E. E. Evans-Pritchard, eds., *African Political Systems* (New York: KPI in association with the International African Institute, 1987). For further information on the arrival and distribution of ethnic communities in Zambia, see W. V. Brelsford, *The Tribes of Zambia* (Lusaka: Government Printer, 1956).

5. They served as the gateway to South and southeastern Asia, which contained the richest portions of Europe's empires.

6. N. Leys, *Kenya* (London: Hogarth Press, 1924); W. M. Ross, *Kenya from Within: A Short Political History* (London: George Allen and Unwin, 1927); E. A. Brett, *Colonialism and Underdevelopment in East Africa* (London: Heinemann, 1973); R. Wolff, *The Economics of Colonialism: Britain and Kenya, 1870–1930* (New Haven: Yale University Press, 1974); B. Berman and J. Lonsdale, *Unhappy Valley: Conflict in Kenya and Africa* (London: J. Currey, 1992).

7. L. S. B. Leakey, *The Southern Kikuyu before 1903* (London: Academic Press, 1977).

8. See, for example, W. R. Ochieng, *An Outline of the History of the Rift Valley* (Nairobi: East African Literature Bureau, 1975). The group took the name of the language they shared. In contrast to Zambia, we have little information that enables us to assign confident estimates of the dates of these migrations. In Zambia, such estimates have been based on oral histories, in which references may be made to eclipses,

droughts, pandemics, and so forth. Such histories tend to be produced in politically centralized societies, where claims to birthright or status are consequential. Kenya is virtually devoid of kings or paramount chiefs, save for those later conjured up and installed by the colonial government.

9. Since the period discussed herein, new mines have been opened and new cities formed.

10. The boards overlapped and interpenetrated. Among the many excellent studies of Katanga, see J. Libois-Gerard, *Katanga Secession* (Madison: University of Wisconsin Press, 1966); C. Young, *Politics in the Congo* (Princeton: Princeton University Press, 1965). See also S. Hempstone, *Rebels, Mercenaries, & Dividends: The Katanga Story* (New York: Praeger, 1962).

11. I. Cunnison, *History on the Luapula* (London: Oxford University Press for the Rhodes-Livingstone Institute, 1951); R. H. Bates, "Ethnicity and Modernization in Contemporary Africa," Social Science Working Paper No. 16 (Pasadena: Division of Humanities and Social Sciences, California Institute of Technology, 1972).

12. Bates, *Rural Responses to Industrialization*, 322.

13. Ibid. The investment was worth more than any other available in the valley. Because of the presence of the tsetse fly, cattle could not be raised there.

14. For purposes of illustration, I assume the migrant is a male. Indeed, in Luapula, most labor migrants were young males. See the review of the demographic data contained in Bates, *Rural Responses to Industrialization*.

15. M. P. Cowen, "Capital and Household Production: The Case of Wattle in Kenya's Central Province, 1903-1964," in *Anthropology* (Cambridge: Cambridge University Press, 1978); see also G. Kitching, *Class and Economic Change in Kenya* (New Haven: Yale University Press, 1980).

16. B. A. Ogot, "Revolt of the Elders: An Anatomy of the Loyalist Crowd in the Mau Mau Uprising, 1952-1956," in *Hadith 4: Politics and Nationalism in Colonial Kenya*, ed. B. A. Ogot (Nairobi: East African Publishing House, 1972).

17. Important sources include J. Kenyatta, *Facing Mount Kenya* (London: Secker and Warburg, 1953); H. E. Lambert, *Kikuyu Social and Political Institutions* (London: Oxford University Press, 1956); M. P. K. Sorrenson, *Land Reform in Kikuyu Country* (Oxford: Oxford University Press, 1967); Leakey, *The Southern Kikuyu before 1903*; Bates, *Beyond the Miracle of the Market*. Important too is G. Kershaw, "The Land Is the People" (unpublished manuscript).

18. The account that follows draws from Bates, *Beyond the Miracle of the Market*.

19. By 1947, more than one-sixth of the Kikuyu people were squatters. See Colony and Protectorate of Kenya, *A Discussion of the Problems of the Squatter* (Nairobi: Government Printer, 1947), 3, 4. See also T. Kanongo, *Squatters and the Roots of Mau Mau, 1905-1963* (London: James Currey, 1987).

20. Cowen, "Capital and Household Production."

21. J. Spencer, *The KAU: The Kenya African Union* (London: KPI, 1985); D. Anderson, *Histories of the Hanged: The Dirty War in Kenya and the End of Empire* (New York: W. W. Norton, 2005).

22. Kenyatta, *Facing Mount Kenya.*

23. Kenyatta was not involved in the making of this decision. From Koinange's point of view, he was an agent, not a principal, and had no "need to know."

24. Circa 1960, the white population was roughly 7 percent of the population of Southern Rhodesia (now Zambia), 3 percent of that in Northern Rhodesia (now Zambia), and less than 1 percent of that in Nyasaland (now Malawi). By restricting the right to vote and thus the size and composition of the electorate, the white minority was able to dominate the governments of the three territories and of the Federation.

25. The portions of the Copperbelt that backed ANC, such as Mufulira, drew a large portion of their population from Central Province. D. H. Davies, *Zambia in Maps* (London: University of London Press, 1971).

26. See the discussions in Libois-Gerard, *Katanga Secession* and Hempstone, *Rebels, Mercenaries, and Dividends.*

27. They proposed including Barotse as well, as the mining companies in Zambia had acquired their mineral rights by signing a treaty with the Litunga, or paramount chief, of the Lozi. See A. Sardanis, *Zambia: The First 50 Years* (New York: I. B. Tauris, 2014). See also D. C. Mulford, *Northern Rhodesia General Election, 1962* (Oxford: Oxford University Press, 1964); D. C. Mulford, *Zambia: The Politics of Independence, 1957–1964* (Oxford: Oxford University Press, 1967).

28. They were of course familiar with the manner in which co-nationals were treated in the mines in South Africa.

29. Bates, *Unions, Parties and Political Development*; see also M. Mwendapole, *A History of the Trade Union Movement up to 1968* (Lusaka: University of Zambia, Institute for African Studies, 1977); S. Zelniker, *Changing Patterns of Trade Unionism: The Zambian Case, 1948–1964* (Ann Arbor, MI: University Microfilms, 1981); J. Prapart, *Labour and Capital in the African Copperbelt* (Philadelphia: Temple University Press, 1983).

30. From reports contained in the files of the mining companies and in the notes taken by David Mulford from the files of the intelligence services.

31. And enabling him to collect taxes from them.

32. In this paragraph, when referring to Mwata, I have adopted the Lunda practice of referring to the title rather than to the incumbent. The title is regarded as perpetual; the incumbent, as transient.

33. Including a Ford Fairlane, which long stood on exhibit in front of Kazembe's palace.

34. It should be noted that Roan Antelope is the mine closest to the valley and that a major portion of its workforce was drawn from Luapula.

35. In the course of my fieldwork, I was told several stories of this kind. Their self-glorifying nature and the theatrical manner in which they were narrated initially made me skeptical of them. It was only when I went through David Mulford's notes that I found them confirmed—all, that is, save this. Having earlier been compelled to revise my assessment of my narrators' veracity, I am now willing to place this account in print.

36. Interviews suggest and documents confirm that they took inspiration from events in Kenya and sought to emulate the activists there.

Chapter 6: The Use of Power

1. More specifically, the Central Committee of UNIP, for reasons that will become apparent.

2. Sorrenson, *Land Reform in Kikuyu Country*.

3. See the sources contained in Bates, *Beyond the Miracle of the Market*.

4. For analyses of this period, see G. Wasserman, *The Politics of Decolonization* (New York: Cambridge University Press, 1976); A. K. Onoma, *The Politics of Property Rights Institutions in Africa* (New York: Cambridge University Press, 2010); C. Boone, "Politically Allocated Land Rights and the Geography of Electoral Violence: The Case of Kenya in the 1990s" (paper prepared for the Annual Meetings of the American Political Science Association, Boston, 2008); Jennifer Widner, *The Rise of a Party State in Kenya: From "Harembe!" to "Nyayo"* (Berkeley: University of California Press, 1992).

5. W. Tordoff, ed., *The Politics of Zambia* (Manchester: Manchester University Press, 1974); R. H. Bates and P. Collier, "The Case of Zambia," in *Political and Economic Interactions in Economic Policy Reform*, ed. R. H. Bates and A. O. Krueger (Oxford: Blackwell, 1993).

6. Unlike proconsuls, however, they could not legally impose "high justice"; that right remained in the hands of the courts.

7. Bates, *Unions, Parties and Political Development*. The best study of the party remains M. R. Bates, "UNIP in Postindependence Zambia" (PhD diss., Department of Government, Harvard University, 1971).

8. In the lexicon of liberation movements.

9. While I was working in Zambia, the average population density was roughly twelve people per square mile; as urban populations are included in this estimate, the figure for the rural areas was far smaller.

10. Much of this material is drawn from R. H. Bates, *Mineworkers in Zambia* (New Haven: Yale University Press, 1969); Bates, *Rural Responses to Industrialization*.

11. R. H. Bates, *Markets and States in Tropical Africa* (Berkeley: University of California Press, 1981), 94–95.

12. Which it did very ably, on average securing for Kenya's smallholders 95 percent of the price in world markets.

13. For a review, see Bates, *Beyond the Miracle of the Market*.

14. D. J. Dodge, *Agricultural Policy and Performance in Zambia* (Berkeley: Institute of International Studies, University of California, 1977).

15. And therefore the conditions under which Kenya achieved independence.

16. When he later retired from politics, Moi possessed seven homes, a fleet of automobiles, and thirty "major business firms" (BBC, Africa Service, July 30, 2002). As documented by auditors later charged with investigating corruption in Kenya, one son—Gideon—owned farmlands and commercial property, both in the capital and on the coast of Kenya; properties in England, Italy, and South Africa; and holdings in banks, airlines, and television stations in East Africa. Phillip, the president's second

son, reportedly owned hotels and lodges in Kenya and bank accounts totaling over $700 million in Britain, Italy, Switzerland, and Brunei. The report documents as well Moi's financial ties with Nicolas Biwott and others of Moi's political associates in the Rift. KTM Confidential Report (Kroll Associates), http://wikileaks.org.

17. Mostly located in what were known as the second-class trading areas of Zambia's urban centers.

18. Zambia Industrial and Mining Corporation.

19. Industrial Development Corporation.

20. It is difficult not to see this as an example of the argument put forward by B. D. Bernheim and M. P. Whinston, "Menu Auctions, Resource Allocation, and Economic Influence," *Quarterly Journal of Economics* 101, no. 1 (1986): 1–31.

21. See the account in Bates, *Rural Responses to Industrialization*.

22. For additional evidence, see M. Bratton, *The Local Politics of Rural Development: Peasant and Party State in Zambia* (Hanover, NH: University Press of New England, 1980); M. Larmer, "'A Little Bit Like a Volcano': The United Progressive Party and Resistance to One-Party Rule in Zambia, 1964–1980," *International Journal of African Historical Studies* 39, no. 1 (2006): 49–83.

23. Sardanis, *Zambia*, 45.

24. When Kaunda reversed his position regarding the outcome of the intraparty elections, he cost the senior Lozi leaders their seats in the Central Committee. They therefore stood ready to take Western Province out of UNIP. Recall that Zambia then contained nine provinces. In an election, the dissidents could now plausibly win five of them.

25. Several of their critiques were published in "Kenya: The Agrarian Question," *Review of African Political Economy* 1, no. 20 (1981).

26. See J. Barry, "Elephants, Charcoal," *The Sunday Times*, 1975; J. Barry, "How Jomo's Royal Family Grabbed the Nation's Wealth," *The Sunday Times*, 1975; J. Barry, "Kenya on the Brink," *The Sunday Times*, 1975.

27. The creation of the Kenya People's Union took place at a time when both China and the Soviet Union were making inroads into East and Central Africa. Kenyatta's efforts to dismantle the KPU therefore received logistical and political backing from Western embassies. C. Hornsby, *Kenya: A History since Independence* (New York: I. B. Tauris, 2013). For insight into the impact of inequality (inter- as well as intraregional) on Kenyan politics, see "Kenya: The Agrarian Question in Kenya," 8; G. Lamb, *Peasant Politics: Conflict and Development in Murang'a* (Sussex: Julian Friedmann, 1974). See also International Labour Office, "Employment, Incomes and Equality: A Strategy for Increasing Productive Employment in Kenya" (Geneva: International Labor Organization, 1972); C. Leys, "Interpreting African Underdevelopment: Reflections on the ILO Report on Employment, Incomes and Equality in Kenya," *African Affairs* 72, no. 289 (1973): 419–29. Heated controversies over regional inequality and regional distribution arose following this report. The issue remains topical today. E.g., consult R. Burgess, R. Jedwab, et al., *Our Turn to Eat: The Political Economy of Roads in Kenya* (London: STICRED London School of Economics, 2010).

28. See C. Morris, *A Humanist in Africa* (Nashville: Abingdon Press, 1966).

29. Bates and Collier, "The Case of Zambia"; I. Mwanawina and J. Mulungushi, "Zambia," in *The Political Economy of Economic Growth in Africa, 1960–2000*, ed. B. Ndulu et al. (New York: Cambridge University Press, 2008).

30. Constant 1994 U.S. dollars. M. J. Ellyne, "Zambia's Economic History" (Washington, DC: International Monetary Fund, 2002), table 1.

31. R. H. Bates, B. Weingast, and R. de Figueiredo, "The Politics of Interpretation, Rationality and Culture," *Politics and Society* 26, no. 4 (1998): 603–42.

32. The Parliamentary Select Committee appointed to investigate the assassination made explicit mention of Peter Mbiyu Koinange, while not detailing his role in the events surrounding it. See as well *The Daily Post*, April 15, 2013, http://www.kenyan-post.com/2013/04/detailed-report-on-how-kenyatta-killed.html. Kariuki was not the only one of Kenyatta's opponents to suffer this fate. See also the description of the death of Pio Gama Pinto in Hornsby, *Kenya*.

33. Albeit with some difficulty (and luck). See J. Karimi and W. R. Ochieng, *The Kenyatta Succession* (Nairobi: Transafrica, 1980).

34. See D. Throup and C. Hornsby, eds., *Multiparty Politics in Kenya* (Athens: Ohio University Press, 1998). For greater depth and detail, see A. Harris, "Three Essays on Politics in Kenya" (PhD diss., Department of Government, Harvard University, 2012) and S. D. Mueller, "The Political Economy of Kenya's Crisis," *Journal of Eastern African Studies* 2, no. 2 (2008): 185–210. KTM Confidential Report (Kroll Associates), http://wikileaks.org, 22. No less telling, on the streets of Nairobi, Biwott became known as "Total Man," a phrase alluding to his ownership of an eponymous chain of petrol stations as well as his ability to dominate every arena, be it in business or politics. Africa Watch, *Divide and Rule: State-Sponsored Ethnic Violence in Kenya* (New York: Human Rights Watch, 1993); L. Mulli, *Understanding Election Clashes in Kenya, 1992 and 1997* (London: Africa Watch, 1998); *Inter-Parties Task Force Report*, June 11, 1992; Government of Kenya, *Report of the Commission of Inquiry into the Illegal/Irregular Allocation of Public Land (Ndungu Land Commission)* (Nairobi, 2004).

35. See Bates, *Rural Responses to Industrialization*, chapter 11.

Chapter 7: Conclusion

1. If one eliminates petrol states and states with economies based on the provision of financial services.

2. Pace the claims of C. Johnson, *MITI and the Japanese Miracle* (Stanford: Stanford University Press, 1982) or J. E. Campos and H. Root, *The Key to the Asian Miracle* (Washington, DC: Brookings Institution, 1996).

3. R. D. Luce and H. Raiffa, *Games and Decisions* (New York: John Wiley and Sons, 1957); W. H. Riker and P. C. Ordeshook, *An Introduction to Positive Political Theory* (New York: Prentice Hall, 1973). To be noted is that the logic of the divide the dollar game applies not only to the capture of benefits but also to the apportionment of costs. Thus the discussion of the problems faced by the French monarch when apportioning the costs of defense (see chapter 4).

4. This analysis applies not only to efforts to secure the benefits of government spending but also to efforts to elude the costs and to shift the burden onto others. Thus the analysis of tax avoidance in chapter 3.

5. S. M. Lipset, *Political Man* (Garden City, NY: Doubleday, 1960); J. Goldstone, M. Marshall, et al., *State Failure Task Force Project, Phase III Report* (McLean, VA: SAIC, 2003).

6. One is reminded of the arguments of Bernheim and Whinston, "Menu Auctions, Resource Allocation, and Political Influence." For an application of their theory to politics, see E. Helpman and G. M. Grossman, *Special Interest Politics* (Cambridge, MA: MIT Press, 2001).

7. See J.-P. Azam, "The Political Geography of Redistribution," in *The Political Economy of Economic Growth in Africa*, ed. B. J. Ndulu, S. A. O'Connell, R. H. Bates, P. Collier, and C. C. Saludo (New York: Cambridge University Press, 2008).

8. N. Sambanis and H. Hegre, "Sensitivity Analysis of Empirical Results on Civil War Onset," *Journal of Conflict Resolution* 50, no. 4 (2006): 508–35.

9. See V. C. Uchendu, *The Igbo of Southeast Nigeria* (New York: Holt, Rinehart, and Winston, 1965); D. Abernethy, *The Political Dilemma of Popular Education: An African Case Study* (Stanford: Stanford University Press, 1969); A. F. Hershfield, "Ibo Sons Abroad: A Window on the World" (paper presented at Annual Meetings of the African Studies Association, Montreal, 1969).

10. See M. Weiner, *Sons of the Soil: Migration and Ethnic Conflict in India* (Princeton: Princeton University Press, 1978); P. Brass, ed., *Ethnic Groups and the State* (London: Croom, Helm, 1985); A. Varshney, *Ethnic Conflict and Civil Life* (New Haven: Yale University Press, 2002); S. I. Wilkinson, *Votes and Violence* (New York: Cambridge University Press, 2004); Y. Tajima, *The Institutional Origins of Communal Violence* (New York: Cambridge University Press, 2014).

11. See D. Horowitz, *Ethnic Groups in Conflict* (Berkeley: University of California Press, 1985); Tajima, *The Institutional Origins of Communal Violence*.

12. Wilkinson, *Votes and Violence*.

13. For an example, turn to the opening sections of Uchendu, *The Igbo of Southeast Nigeria*.

14. The late Peter Ekeh provided a powerful account of this phenomenon: P. Ekeh, "Colonialism and the Two Publics in Africa," *Contemporary Studies in Society and History* 17, no. 1 (1975): 91–112.

15. Montalvo and Reynal-Querol, "Ethnic Polarization, Potential Conflict, and Civil Wars"; J. A. Goldstone et al., "A Global Model for Forecasting Political Instability," *American Journal of Political Science* 54, no. 1 (January 2010): 190–208; L.-E. Cederman, K. S. Gleditsch, et al., *Inequality, Grievances, and Civil War* (New York: Cambridge University Press, 2013).

16. Apter, *Old Societies and New States*; M. C. Young, *The Rising Tide of Cultural Pluralism* (Madison: University of Wisconsin Press, 1983); Coleman and Rosberg, *Political Parties and National Integration*.

17. I refer in particular to E. R. Wolf, *Peasant Wars of the Twentieth Century* (New

York: Harper and Row, 1969); B. Moore, *Social Origins of Dictatorship and Democracy* (Boston: Beacon Press, 1966); J. C. Scott, *The Moral Economy of the Peasant* (New Haven: Yale University Press, 1976). For a review of this literature, see R. H. Bates, "Agrarian Politics," in *Understanding Political Development*, ed. M. Weiner, S. P. Huntington, and G. Almond (Boston: Little, Brown, 1987).

18. I refer in particular to Huntington, *Political Order in Changing Societies*.

19. In addition, the force of Huntington's arguments convinces us of their merits; mine acquire cogency—I hope—through formal proof or statistical demonstration. See the addendum to chapter 2 and to this chapter.

20. North, Wallis, et al., *Violence and Social Orders*; Acemoglu and Robinson, *Why Nations Fail*; see also J.-L. Rosenthal and R. B. Wong, *Before and Beyond Divergence: Institutions and Prosperity in China and Europe, 1000–1800* (Cambridge, MA: Harvard University Press, 2011); P. T. Hoffman, *Why Did Europe Conquer the World?* (Princeton: Princeton University Press, 2015).

21. At least formal ones.

22. Cederman, Gleditsch, et al., *Inequality, Grievances, and Civil War*.

23. For definitions of these terms and references to the relevant sources, refer to the addendum to this chapter.

24. Sambanis and Hegre, "Sensitivity Analysis of Empirical Results on Civil War Onset." See also the tables appearing in the addendum to this chapter.

25. Let the growth rate over the next ten years be for the first economy: 5,5,5,5,5,5,5,5,5,5,; for the second, 8, –10, 8, –7, 8, –4, 15, 10, 12, 10. For further discussion, see L. Pritchett, "Understanding Patterns of Economic Growth: Searching for Hills among Plateaus, Mountains, and Plains," *World Bank Economic Review* 14, no. 2 (2000): 221–50. See also D. Rodrik, "Where Did All the Growth Go? External Shocks, Social Conflict, and Growth Collapses," *Journal of Economic Growth* 4, no. 4 (1999): 385–412.

Addendum to Chapter 2

1. This section is abstracted from Bates, Greif, et al., "Organizing Violence."

2. D. Fudenberg and E. Maskin, "The Folk Theorem in Repeated Games with Discounting or with Incomplete Information," *Econometrica* 54, no. 3 (1986): 533–54.

3. For a response to this question, see Bates, R. H., D. Soskice, et al. "Ambition and Constraint: The Stabilizing Role of Institutions." *The Journal of Law, Economics, and Organization* 8, no. 3 (1992): 547–60.

Addendum to Chapter 6

1. Max Weber, "Ethnicity," in *Economy and Society*, ed. Guenter Roth and Claus Wittich (Berkeley: University of California Press, 1968).

2. See, for example, Brelsford, *The Tribes of Zambia*; B. A. Ogot, ed., *Kenya before 1900* (Nairobi: East African Publishing House, 1978).

3. See the chapter by J. E. G. Sutton in Ogot, *Kenya before 1900*; see also G. Lynch, *I Say to You: Ethnic Politics and the Kalenjin in Kenya* (Chicago: University of Chicago Press, 2011). Note the similarity with the history of the Franks. See, e.g., Tacitus, *Agricola and Germany* (Oxford: Oxford University Press, 1999); Gregory of Tours, *History of the Franks* (New York: Penguin Classics, 1974); G. Hallsall, ed., *Barbarian Migrations and the Roman West* (New York: Cambridge University Press, 2007), 376–568.

4. The case is narrated and discussed in D. W. Cohen and E. S. A. Odhiambo, *Burying SM* (Portsmouth: Heinemann, 1992).

5. The following account is drawn from M. Wrong, *It's Our Turn to Eat* (New York: HarperCollins, 2009).

6. Ibid., 152.

7. Francis Fukuyama advances a similar line of argument in *The Origins of Political Order* (New York: Farrar, Straus and Giroux, 2011). Refer as well to Duby, *Medieval Marriage*; Duby, *The Knight, the Lady, and the Priest*; and Goody, *The Development of the Family and Marriage in Europe*.

Addendum to Chapter 7

1. Zambia quite comfortably, Kenya just barely. Data from the World Bank's World Development Indictors, http://data.worldbank.org/products/wdi.

2. Here and elsewhere in this addendum, I classify as developing countries those that once were colonies.

3. Sixty-six percent of the nations that once were colonies exhibit high levels of polarization.

4. See the notes to the tables in this addendum. When Hariri constructed his index, he used settler population as an instrument, which may account for the higher than expected scores for these two countries.

5. But less likely to experience riots and demonstrations. Entry into and exit from office is judged irregular when it "fails to take place in accord [with the polity's] explicit rules or established conventions." Archigos codebook: www.rochester.edu /college/faculty/hgoemans/Archigo2.9.

6. And if exhibiting regional inequality, a high frequency of riots and demonstrations as well.

7. See also Pritchett, "Understanding Patterns of Economic Growth."

8. Economists who study the relationship between political and economic growth often regress political shocks against growth rates averaged over five-year periods. By failing to take into account the duration of the impact of political shocks, they secure invalid estimates of their impact on economic performance.

9. Note the earlier contribution of Rodrik, "Where Did All the Growth Go?"

10. Save for regional inequality.

BIBLIOGRAPHY

Abernethy, D. *The Dynamics of Global Dominance: European Overseas Empires, 1415–1980*. New Haven: Yale University Press, 2000.

———. *The Political Dilemma of Popular Education: An African Case Study*. Stanford: Stanford University Press, 1969.

Abu-Lughod, J. L. *Before European Hegemony: The World System A.D. 1250–1350*. Oxford: Oxford University Press, 1989.

Acemoglu, D., and J. Robinson. *Why Nations Fail*. New York: Crown, 2012.

Acemoglu, D., J. A. Robinson, et al. "The Colonial Origins of Comparative Development." *American Economic Review* 91, no. 5 (2001): 1369–1401.

Africa Watch. *Divide and Rule: State-Sponsored Ethnic Violence in Kenya*. New York: Human Rights Watch, 1993.

Alesina, A., and E. Spolare. *The Size of Nations*. Cambridge, MA: MIT Press, 2003.

Allen, D. S. *The World of Prometheus: The Politics of Punishing in Democratic Athens*. Princeton: Princeton University Press, 2002.

Allen, R. C. *The British Industrial Revolution in Global Perspective*. New York: Cambridge University Press, 2009.

———. "The Nitrogen Hypothesis and the English Agricultural Revolution: A Biological Analysis." *Journal of Economic History* 68 (2008): 182–210.

Anderson, C. W., F. R. von der Mehden, et al. *Issues of Political Development*. Englewood Cliffs, NJ: Prentice-Hall, 1967.

Anderson, D. *Histories of the Hanged: The Dirty War in Kenya and the End of Empire*. New York: W. W. Norton, 2005.

Appleby, J. T. *The Troubled Reign of King Stephen*. London: G. Bell and Sons, 1969.

Apter, D., ed. *Old Societies and New States*. New York: Free Press of Glencoe, 1963.

Ausenda, G., ed. *After Empire: Towards an Ethnology of Europe's Barbarians*. Studies in Historical Archaeoethnology. Woodbridge: Boydell Press, 1995.

Azam, J.-P. "The Political Geography of Redistribution." In *The Political Economy of Economic Growth in Africa*, ed. B. J. Ndulu, S. A. O'Connell, R. H. Bates, P. Collier, and C. C. Saludo. New York: Cambridge University Press, 2008.

———. "The Redistributive State and Conflicts in Africa." *Journal of Peace Research* 38, no. 4 (2001): 429–44.

Azam, J.-P., R. H. Bates, et al. "Political Predation and Economic Development." *Economics and Politics* 2, no. 2 (2009): 255–77.

Azam, J.-P., and A. Mesnard. "Civil War and the Social Contract." *Public Choice* 115 (2003): 455–75.

Baldwin, J. W. *The Government of Philip Augustus*. Berkeley: University of California Press, 1986.

Baldwin, R. E. *Economic Development and Export Growth: A Study of Northern Rhodesia, 1920–1960*. Berkeley: University of California Press, 1966.

Barber, W. J. *The Economy of British Central Africa*. London: Oxford University Press, 1961.

Barraclough, G. *The Crucible of Europe: The Ninth and Tenth Centuries in European History*. Berkeley: University of California Press, 1976.

Bastable, C. *Public Finance*. London: Macmillan, 1917.

Bates, M. R. "UNIP in Postindependence Zambia." PhD diss., Harvard University, Department of Government, 1971.

Bates, R. H. "Agrarian Politics." In *Understanding Political Development*, ed. M. Weiner, S. P. Huntington, and G. Almond. Boston: Little, Brown, 1987.

——. *Analytic Narratives*. Princeton: Princeton University Press, 1998.

——. *Beyond the Miracle of the Market*. Cambridge: Cambridge University Press, 1989.

——. "Capital, Kinship, and Conflict." *Canadian Journal of African Studies* 24, no. 2 (1990): 151–64.

——. "The Case of Zambia." In *Political and Economic Interactions in Economic Policy Reform*, ed. R. H. Bates and A. O. Krueger. Oxford: Blackwell, 1993.

——. "Ethnicity and Modernization in Contemporary Africa." Social Science Working Paper No. 16. Pasadena: Division of Humanities and Social Sciences, California Institute of Technology, 1972.

——. "Kenya: The Agrarian Question." *Review of African Political Economy* 1, no. 20 (1981).

——. "Lessons from History, or the Perfidy of English Exceptionalism and the Significance of Historical France," *World Politics* 40, no. 4 (1988): 499–516

——. *Markets and States in Tropical Africa*. Berkeley: University of California Press, 1981.

——. *Mineworkers in Zambia*. New Haven: Yale University Press, 1969.

——. *Rural Responses to Industrialization*. New Haven: Yale University Press, 1976.

——. *Unions, Parties, and Political Development*. New Haven: Yale University Press, 1971.

Bates, R. H., and P. Collier. "The Case of Zambia." In *Political and Economic Interactions in Economic Policy Reform*, edited by R. H. Bates and A. O. Krueger. Oxford: Blackwell, 1991.

Bates, R. H., A. Greif, et al. "Organizing Violence." *Journal of Conflict Resolution* 46, no. 5 (October 2002): 599–628.

Bates, R. H., D. Soskice, et al. "Ambition and Constraint: The Stabilizing Role of Institutions." *The Journal of Law, Economics and Organization* 8, no. 3 (1992): 547–60.

Bates, R. H., B. Weingast, and R. de Figueiredo. "The Politics of Interpretation, Rationality and Culture." *Politics and Society* 26, no. 4 (1998): 603–42.

Beckert, S. *Empire of Cotton*. New York: Alfred A. Knopf, 2014.

Beik, W. *Absolutism and Society in Seventeenth-Century France: State Power and*

Provincial Aristocracy in Languedoc. New York: Cambridge University Press, 1989.

Benton, J. F., ed. *Town Origins: The Evidence from Medieval England.* Lexington, MA: D. C. Heath, 1968.

Berman, B., and J. Lonsdale. *Unhappy Valley: Conflict in Kenya and Africa.* London: J. Currey, 1992.

Berman, H. J. *Law and Revolution: The Formation of the Western Legal Tradition.* Cambridge, MA: Harvard University Press, 1988.

Bernheim, B. D., and M. P. Whinston. "Menu Auctions, Resource Allocation, and Economic Influence." *Quarterly Journal of Economics* 101, no. 1 (1986): 1–32.

Bien, D. "Les offices, les corps et le credit d'état." *Annales* 43 (1988): 379–404.

Bisson, T. N. *The Crisis of the Twelfth Century.* Princeton: Princeton University Press, 2009.

Bloch, M. *Feudal Society.* Chicago: University of Chicago Press, 1970.

Boehm, C. *Blood Revenge.* Philadelphia: University of Pennsylvania Press, 1984.

Bogart, D. "Turnpike Trusts and Property Income." *Economic History Review* 62, no. 1 (2009): 128–52.

———. "Turnpike Trusts and the Transportation Revolution in Eighteenth Century England." *Explorations in Economic History* 65 (2005): 439–68.

Boone, C. "Politically Allocated Land Rights and the Geography of Electoral Violence: The Case of Kenya in the 1990s." Paper prepared for the Annual Meetings of the American Political Science Association, Boston, 2008.

———. *Political Topographies of the African State: Rural Authority and Institutional Choice.* Cambridge: Cambridge University Press, 2003.

Boserup, E. *The Conditions of Agricultural Growth.* London: G. Allen and Unwin, 1965.

Boulger, D. *The History of Belgium: Part 1—Caesar to Waterloo.* Laurel, MD: Elibron Classics, 2005.

Bradbury, J. *Stephen and Matilda: The Civil War of 1339–53.* Summerset, Fromme: Alan Sutton Publishing, 1996.

Brass, P., ed. *Ethnic Groups and the State.* London: Croom, Helm, 1985.

Bratton, M. *The Local Politics of Rural Development: Peasant and Party State in Zambia.* Hanover, NH: University Press of New England, 1980.

Brelsford, W. V. *The Tribes of Zambia.* Lusaka: Government Printer, 1956.

Brendon, P. *The Decline and Fall of the British Empire, 1781–1997.* New York: Vintage, 2007.

Brenner, R. "Agrarian Class Structure and Economic Development in Pre-Industrial Europe." *Past and Present* 70 (February 1976): 30–75.

———. *Merchants and Revolution: Commercial Change, Political Conflict, and London's Overseas Traders, 1550–1653.* Princeton: Princeton University Press, 1993.

Brett, E. A. *Colonialism and Underdevelopment in East Africa.* London: Heinemann, 1973.

Brewer, J. *The Sinews of Power: War, Money and the English State, 1688–1783.* New York: Knopf, 1988.

Burgess, R., R. Jedwab, et al., *Our Turn to Eat: The Political Economy of Roads in Kenya*. London: STICRED, London School of Economics, 2010.

Campos, J. E., and H. Root. *The Key to the Asian Miracle*. Washington, DC: Brookings Institution, 1996.

Cederman, L.-E., K. S. Gleditsch, et al. *Inequality, Grievances, and Civil War*. New York: Cambridge University Press, 2013.

Chandler, T., and G. Fox. *3000 Years of Urban Growth*. New York: Academic Press, 1974.

Chenery, H. B., and L. Taylor. "Development Patterns: Among Countries and over Time." *Review of Economics and Statistics* 50, no. 4 (November 1968): 391–416.

Cohen, D. W., and E. S. A. Odhiambo. *Burying SM*. Portsmouth: Heinemann, 1992.

Coleman, D. C. "Proto-Industrialization: A Concept Too Many." *Economic History Review* 36, no. 3 (1983): 435–88.

Coleman, J. S., and C. G. Rosberg. *Political Parties and National Integration*. Berkeley: University of California Press, 1964.

Colony and Protectorate of Kenya. *A Discussion of the Problems of the Squatter*. Nairobi: Government Printer, 1947.

Colson, E. *Tradition and Contract: The Problem of Order*. Chicago: Aldine, 1974.

Cowen, M. P. "Capital and Household Production: The Case of Wattle in Kenya's Central Province, 1903–1964." PhD diss., Cambridge University, 1978.

Cunnison, I. *History on the Luapula*. London: Oxford University Press for the Rhodes-Livingstone Institute, 1951.

Davies, D. H. *Zambia in Maps*. London: University of London Press, 1971.

Davis, J. M. *Modern Industry and the African*. London: Macmillan, 1933.

Davis, R. H. C. *King Stephen, 1135–1154*. London: Longman, 1990.

———. "What Happened in Stephen's Reign, 1135–1154." *History* 49, no. 165 (1964): 1–12.

Dessert, D., and J.-L. Journet. "Le Lobby Colbert: Un Royaume, ou une affaire de famille?" *Annales* 30, no. 6 (1975): 1303–36.

De Vries, J. *European Urbanization, 1500–1800*. Cambridge, MA: Harvard University Press, 1984.

Devroey, J.-P. "The Economy." In *The Early Middle Ages: Europe, 400–1000*, ed. R. McKitterick, 97–130. Oxford: Oxford University Press, 2003.

Dincecco, M. *Political Transformation and Public Finances: Europe, 1650–1913*. New York: Cambridge University Press, 2011.

Dodge, D. J. *Agricultural Policy and Performance in Zambia*. Berkeley: Institute of International Studies, University of California, 1977.

Downing, B. M. *The Military Revolution and Political Change*. Princeton: Princeton University Press, 1992.

Duby, G. *France in the Middle Ages, 987–1460*. Oxford: Blackwell, 1987.

———. *The Knight, the Lady, and the Priest: The Making of Modern Marriage in Medieval France*. Chicago: University of Chicago Press, 1981.

———. *Medieval Marriage: Two Models from Twelfth-Century France*. Baltimore: Johns Hopkins University Press, 1978.

Edwards, J., and S. Ogilvie. "What Lessons for Economic Development Can We Draw from the Champagne Fairs?" *Journal of Economic History* 49 (2012): 131–48.

Ekeh, P. "Colonialism and the Two Publics in Africa: A Theoretical Statement." *Contemporary Studies in Society and History* 17, no. 1 (January 1975): 91–112.

Ellyne, M. J. "Zambia's Economic History." Washington, DC: International Monetary Fund, 2002.

Emerson, R. *From Empire to Nation*. Boston, Beacon Press, 1962.

Epstein, S. A. *An Economic and Social History of Later Medieval Europe, 1000–1500*. New York: Cambridge University Press, 2009.

Fearon, J. D., and D. D. Laitin. "Explaining Interethnic Cooperation." *American Political Science Review* 90 (December 1996): 715–35.

Finlay, R., and K. H. O'Rourke. *Power and Plenty: Trade, War and the World Economy in the Second Millennium*. Princeton: Princeton University Press, 2009.

Firmin-Sellers, K. *The Transformation of Property Rights in the Gold Coast: An Empirical Study Applying Rational Choice Theory*. Cambridge: Cambridge University Press, 1996.

Fletcher, R. *Blood Feud*. Oxford: Oxford University Press, 2003.

Fontescue, S. J. *The Governance of England*. Oxford: Oxford University Press, 1885.

Fortes, M., and E. E. Evans-Pritchard, eds. *African Political Systems*. New York: KPI in association with the International African Institute, 1987.

Fried, M. *The Notion of the Tribe*. Menlo Park, CA: Cummings Publishing, 1975.

Fudenberg, D., and E. Maskin. "The Folk Theorem in Repeated Games with Discounting or with Incomplete Information." *Econometrica* 54, no. 3 (1986): 533–54.

Fukuyama, Francis. *The Origins of Political Order*. New York: Farrar, Straus and Giroux, 2011.

Gann, L. H. *A History of Northern Rhodesia, Early Days to 1953*. London: Chatto and Windus, 1964.

Geertz, C. "The Integrative Revolution: Primordial Sentiments and Civil Politics in the New States." In *Old Societies and New States*, ed. D. Apter. New York: Free Press of Glencoe, 1963.

Gilbert, F., and R. M. Berdhal, eds. *The Historical Essays of Otto Hintze*. New York: Oxford University Press, 1975.

Gluckman, M. *Custom and Conflict in Africa*. Oxford: Blackwell, 1955.

Goldstone, J. A., R. H. Bates, D. L. Epstein, T. R. Gurr, M. B. Lustik, M. G. Marshall, J. Ulfelder, and M. Woodward. "A Global Model for Forecasting Political Instability." *American Journal of Political Science* 54, no. 1 (January 2010): 190–208.

Goldstone, J., M. Marshall, et al. *State Failure Task Force Project, Phase III Report*. McLean, VA: SAIC, 2003.

Goody, J. *The Development of the Family and Marriage in Europe*. Cambridge: Cambridge University Press, 1983.

Government of Kenya. *Report of the Commission of Inquiry into the Illegal/Irregular Allocation of Public Land (Ndungu Land Commission)*. Nairobi, 2004.

Gregory of Tours. *History of the Franks*. New York: Penguin Classics, 1974.

Halsall, G. *Barbarian Migrations and the Roman West, 376–568*. Cambridge: Cambridge University Press, 2007.

Hardy, M. J. L. *Blood Feuds and the Payment of Blood Money in the Middle East*. Beirut: Catholic Press, 1963.

Hariri, J. G. "The Autocratic Legacy of Early Statehood." *American Political Science Review* 106, no. 3 (2012): 471–94.

Harris, A. "Three Essays on Politics in Kenya." PhD diss., Department of Government, Harvard University, 2012.

Harris, G. L. *King, Parliament, and Public Finance in Medieval England to 1369*. Oxford: Clarendon, 1975.

Head, T., and R. Landes, eds. *The Peace of God*. Ithaca: Cornell University Press, 1992.

Helpman, E., and G. M. Grossman. *Special Interest Politics*. Cambridge, MA: MIT Press, 2001.

Hempstone, S. *Rebels, Mercenaries, & Dividends: The Katanga Story*. New York: Praeger, 1962.

Henneman, J. B. "Nobility, Privilege and Fiscal Politics in Late Medieval France." *French Historical Studies* 13, no. 1 (1983): 1–17.

Herbst, J. *States and Power in Africa*. Princeton: Princeton University Press, 2000.

Hershfield, A. F. "Ibo Sons Abroad: A Window on the World." Paper presented at Annual Meetings of the African Studies Association, Montreal, 1969.

Hirshleifer, J. "The Dark Side of the Force." *Economic Inquiry* 32 (1994): 1–10.

———. *The Dark Side of the Force: The Economic Foundations of Conflict Theory*. New York: Cambridge University Press, 2001.

Hobbes, T. *Leviathan*. Great Political Thinkers, ed. W. Ebenstein. New York: Holt, Reinhart and Winston, 1961.

Hoffman, P. *Growth in a Traditional Society: The French Countryside, 1450–1815*. Princeton: Princeton University Press, 1996.

———. "Institutions and Agriculture in Old Regime France." *Politics and Society* 16, no. 2–3 (1988): 241–64.

———.*Why Did Europe Conquer the World?* Princeton: Princeton University Press, 2015.

Hoffman, P., G. Postel-Vinay, et al. *Priceless Markets: The Political Economy of Credit in Paris, 1660–1870*. Chicago: University of Chicago Press, 2000.

Hogue, A. R. *The Origins of Common Law*. Bloomington: Indiana University Press, 1966.

Hollister, C. W., and J. W. Baldwin. "The Rise of Administrative Kingship: Henry I and Philip Augustus." *American Historical Review* 83, no. 4 (1978): 867–905.

Holmes, G. *The Good Parliament*. Oxford: Clarendon, 1975.

Hornsby, Charles. *Kenya: A History since Independence*. New York: I. B. Tauris, 2013.

Horowitz, D. *Ethnic Groups in Conflict*. Berkeley: University of California Press, 1985.

Hudson, J. *The Formation of the English Common Law*. New York: Longman, 1996.

Huillery, E. "The Black Man's Burden: The Cost of Colonization of French West Africa." *Journal of Economic History* 74, no. 1 (2014): 1–38.

———. *French West Africa: Did Prosperous Areas Fall Behind?* Paris: Paris School of Economics, 2008.

Huntington, S. P. *Political Order in Changing Societies*. New Haven: Yale University Press, 1968.

Johnson, C. *MITI and the Japanese Miracle*. Stanford: Stanford University Press, 1982.

Jones, C. I. *The Facts of Economic Growth*. Stanford: Stanford Graduate School of Business, 2015.

Jones, D. *The Wars of the Roses*. New York: Penguin, 2014.

Kanongo, T. *Squatters and the Roots of Mau Mau, 1905–1963*. London: James Currey, 1987.

Kaplan, S. L. *Bread, Politics and Political Economy in the Reign of Louis XV*. The Hague: Martinus Nijhoff, 1976.

———. *Provisioning Paris: Merchants and Millers in the Grain and Flour Trade during the Eighteenth Century*. 2 vols. Ithaca: Cornell University Press, 1984.

Karimi, J., and W. R. Ochieng. *The Kenyatta Succession*. Nairobi: Transafrica, 1980.

Keen, M. *Chivalry*. New Haven: Yale University Press, 1984.

Kenyatta, J. *Facing Mount Kenya*. London: Secker and Warburg, 1953.

Kershaw, G. "The Land Is the People." Unpublished manuscript.

King, E., ed. *The Anarchy of King Stephen's Reign*. Oxford: Clarendon, 1994.

Kitching, G. *Class and Economic Change in Kenya*. New Haven: Yale University Press, 1980.

Kupperman, K. O., ed. *America in European Consciousness, 1493–1750*. Chapel Hill: University of North Carolina Press for the Institute of Early American History and Culture, 1995.

Kuznets, S. *Modern Economic Growth*. New Haven: Yale University Press, 1966.

Lamb, G. *Peasant Politics: Conflict and Development in Murang'a*. Sussex: Julian Friedmann, 1974.

Lambert, H. E. *Kikuyu Social and Political Institutions*. London: Oxford University Press, 1956.

Lane, F. C. *Venice and History: The Collected Papers of Frederic C. Lane*. Baltimore: Johns Hopkins University Press, 1966.

Lange, M. "British Colonial Legacies and Political Development." *World Development* 32, no. 6 (2004): 905–22.

———. "British Colonial State Legacies and Development Trajectories: A Statistical Analysis of Direct and Indirect Rule." In *States and Development: Historical Antecedents of Stagnation and Advance*, ed. M. Lange and D. Rueschemeyer, 117–39. New York: Palgrave Macmillan, 2005.

Larmer, M. "'A Little Bit Like a Volcano': The United Progressive Party and Resistance to One-Party Rule in Zambia, 1964–1980." *International Journal of African Historical Studies* 39, no. 1 (2006): 49–83.

Leakey, L. S. B. *The Southern Kikuyu before 1903*. London: Academic Press, 1977.

Levi, M. *Of Rule and Revenue*. Berkeley: University of California Press, 1988.

Leys, C. "Interpreting African Underdevelopment: Reflections on the ILO Report on Employment, Incomes, and Equality in Kenya," *African Affairs* 72, no. 289 (1973): 419–29.

Leys, N. *Kenya*. London: Hogarth Press, 1924.

Libois-Gerard, J. *Katanga Secession*. Madison: University of Wisconsin Press, 1966.

Lindert, P. "Historical Patterns of Agricultural Policy." In *Agriculture and the State*, ed. P. Timmer, 29–83. Ithaca: Cornell University Press, 1991.

Lipset, S. M. *Political Man*. Garden City, NY: Doubleday, 1960.

Lipton, M. *Urban Bias*. London: Temple Smith, 1977.

Lopez, R. *The Commercial Revolution of the Middle Ages, 939–1350*. New York: Cambridge University Press, 1976.

Lotter, F. "The Crusading Idea and the Conquest of the Region East of the Elbe." In *Medieval Frontier Societies*, ed. R. Bartlett, 267–306. Oxford: Clarendon, 1989.

Lucas, R. E. "On the Mechanics of Economic Development." *Journal of Monetary Economics* 22 (1988): 3–42.

Luce, R. D., and H. Raiffa. *Games and Decisions*. New York: John Wiley and Sons, 1957.

Lynch, G. *I Say to You: Ethnic Politics and the Kalenjin in Kenya*. Chicago: University of Chicago Press, 2011.

Maddison, A. *The World Economy*. Paris: Organization for Economic Cooperation & Development, 2006.

McCormick, M. *Origins of the European Economy*. New York: Cambridge University Press, 2005.

Meek, C. K. *Land Law and Custom in the Colonies*. London: Oxford University Press, 1949.

Mendels, F. F. "Proto-Industrialization: The First Phase of the Industrialization Process." *Journal of Economic History* 32, no. 1 (1972): 241–61.

Meredith, M. *The Fortunes of Africa: A 5000-Year History of Wealth, Greed, and Endeavor*. New York: Public Affairs, 2014.

Montalvo, J. G., and M. Reynal-Querol. "Discrete Polarization with an Application to the Determinants of Genocide." *Economic Journal* 118 (November 2008): 1835–65.

———. "Ethnic Polarization, Potential Conflict, and Civil Wars." *American Economic Review* 95, no. 3 (2005): 796–816.

Moore, B. *Social Origins of Dictatorship and Democracy*. Boston: Beacon Press, 1966.

Morris, Colin. *A Humanist in Africa*. Nashville: Abingdon Press, 1966.

Mueller, S. D. "The Political Economy of Kenya's Crisis." *Journal of Eastern African Studies* 2, no. 2 (2008): 185–210.

Mulford, D. C. *Northern Rhodesia General Election, 1962*. Oxford: Oxford University Press, 1964.

———. *Zambia: The Politics of Independence, 1957–1964*. Oxford: Oxford University Press, 1967.

Mulli, L. *Understanding Election Clashes in Kenya, 1992 and 1997*. London: Africa Watch, 1998.

Munro, J. H. "The Symbiosis of Towns and Textiles: Urban Institutions and the Changing Fortunes of Cloth Manufacturing in the Low Countries and England, 1270–1570." MPRA Paper No. 11266. Department of Economics, University of Toronto, 1998.

Mwanawina, I., and J. Mulungushi. "Zambia." In *The Political Economy of Economic Growth in Africa, 1960–2000*, ed. B. Ndulu, S. O'Connell, J.-P. Azam, R. H. Bates, A. K. Fosu, J. W. Gunning, and D. Njinkeu. New York: Cambridge University Press, 2008.

Mwendapole, M. *A History of the Trade Union Movement up to 1968*. Lusaka: University of Zambia, Institute for African Studies, 1977.

Nicholas, D. M. "Medieval Urban Origins in Northern Continental Europe." In *Studies in Medieval and Renaissance History*, ed. W. M. Bowsky, 6:55–115. Lincoln: University of Nebraska Press, 1969.

Norberg, K. "The French Fiscal Crisis of 1788 and the Financial Origins of the Revolution of 1789." In *Fiscal Crises, Liberty, and Representative Government, 1450–1789*, ed. P. T. Hoffman and K. Norberg. Stanford: Stanford University Press, 1994.

North, D. C., J. J. Wallis, et al. *Violence and Social Orders*. New York: Cambridge University Press, 2009.

Ochieng, W. R. *An Outline of the History of the Rift Valley*. Nairobi: East African Literature Bureau, 1975.

Ogot, B. A., ed. *Kenya before 1900*. Nairobi: East African Publishing House, 1978.

———. "Revolt of the Elders: An Anatomy of the Loyalist Crowd in the Mau Mau Uprising, 1952–1956." In *Hadith 4: Politics and Nationalism in Colonial Kenya*, ed. B. A. Ogot. Nairobi: East African Publishing House, 1972.

Onoma, A. K. *The Politics of Property Rights Institutions in Africa*. New York: Cambridge University Press, 2010.

Pakenham, T. *The Scramble for Africa: 1876–1912*. London: Weidenfeld and Nicolson, 1991.

Parker, G. *The Military Revolution: Military Innovation and the Rise of the West, 1500–1800*. New York: Cambridge University Press, 1991.

Parker, W. N. and E. L. Jones, eds. *European Peasants and Their Markets*. Princeton: Princeton University Press, 1975.

Perkins, D., S. C. Radelet, et al. *Economics of Development*. New York: W. W. Norton, 2012.

Pincus, S., and J. A. Robinson. "The Glorious Revolution Revisited." In *The New Institutional History: Essays in Honor of Douglass North*, ed. I. Sened. New York: Cambridge University Press, 2013.

Polanyi, K. *The Great Transformation*. Boston: Beacon Press, 1944.

Pollard, A. F. *The Evolution of Parliament*. London: Longman, 1926.

Posner, D., and D. Simon. "Economic Conditions and Incumbent Support in Africa's New Democracies: Evidence from Zambia." *Comparative Political Studies* 35, no. 3 (2002): 313–36

Power, E. *The Wool Trade in English Medieval History*. Oxford: Oxford University Press, 1941.

Prapart, J. *Labour and Capital in the African Copperbelt*. Philadelphia: Temple University Press, 1983.

Prestwich, J. O. "War and Finance in the Anglo-Norman State." *Transactions of the Royal Historical Society*, 5th ser., 4 (1954): 19–54.

Prestwich, M. *War, Politics and Finance under Edward I*. London: Faber and Faber, 1972.

Pritchett, L. "Understanding Patterns of Economic Growth." *World Bank Economic Review* 14, no. 2 (2000): 221–50.

Ricardo, D. *On the Principles of Political Economy and Taxation*. London: John Murray, 1817.

Riker, W. H., and P. C. Ordeshook. *An Introduction to Positive Political Theory*. New York: Prentice Hall, 1973.

Roberts, M. *The Military Revolution, 1560–1660*. Belfast: M. Boyd, 1956.

Rodrik, D. "The Past, Present, and Future of Economic Growth." Global Citizen Foundation, 2013.

———."Where Did All the Growth Go? External Shocks, Social Conflict, and Growth Collapses." *Journal of Economic Growth* 4, no. 4 (1999): 385–412.

Rogan, E. *The Fall of the Ottomans*. New York: Basic Books, 2015.

Rosenthal, J.-L. *The Fruits of Revolution: Property Rights, Litigation, and French Agriculture, 1700–1860*. New York: Cambridge University Press, 1992.

Rosenthal, J.-L., and R. B. Wong. *Before and Beyond Divergence: Institutions and Prosperity in China and Europe, 1000–1800*. Cambridge, MA: Harvard University Press, 2011.

Ross, W. M. *Kenya from Within: A Short Political History*. London: George Allen and Unwin, 1927.

Sahlins, M. "The Segmentary Lineage: An Organization of Predatory Expansion." *American Anthropologist* 63 (1961): 322–45.

———. "Tribal Economies." In *Economic Development and Social Change*, ed. G. Dalton, 43–61. Garden City, NY: Natural History Press for the American Museum of Natural History, 1971.

Sambanis, N., and H. Hegre. "Sensitivity Analysis of Empirical Results on Civil War Onset." *Journal of Conflict Resolution* 50, no. 4 (2006): 508–35.

Sardanis, A. *Zambia: The First 50 Years*. New York: I. B. Tauris, 2014.

Sargent, T. J., and F. O. R. Velde. "Macroeconomic Features of the French Revolution." *Journal of Political Economy* 103, no. 3 (1995): 474–518.

Scott, J. C. *The Moral Economy of the Peasant*. New Haven: Yale University Press, 1976.

Searle, E. *Predatory Kinship and the Creation of Norman Power, 840–1066*. Berkeley: University of California Press, 1988.

Sklar, R. L. *Nigerian Political Parties*. Princeton: Princeton University Press, 1963.

———. "Political Science and National Integration: A Radical Approach." *Journal of Modern African Studies* 5 (May 1967): 1–11.

Smith, A. *An Inquiry into the Nature and Causes of the Wealth of Nations*. Ed. E. Cannan. Chicago: University of Chicago Press, 1976.

Sorrenson, M. P. K. *Land Reform in Kikuyu Country*. Oxford: Oxford University Press, 1967.

Spencer, J. *The KAU: The Kenya African Union*. London: KPI, 1985.

Stenton, F. M. "Presidential Address: English Families and the Norman Conquest." *Transactions of the Royal Historical Society* 26 (1944): 1–12.

Tacitus. *Agricola and Germany*. Oxford: Oxford University Press, 1999.

Tajima, Y. *The Institutional Origins of Communal Violence*. New York: Cambridge University Press, 2014.

Throup, David, and Charles Hornsby, eds. *Multiparty Politics in Kenya*. Athens: Ohio University Press, 1998.

Tilly, C. *Coercion, Capital and European States, AD 900–1990*. Oxford: Oxford University Press, 1990.

——. "War Making and State Making as Organized Crime." In *Bringing the State Back In*, ed. P. Evans, D. Rueschemeyer, and T. Skocpol. Cambridge: Cambridge University Press, 1985.

Timmer, C. P., and W. P. Falcon. *Food Policy Analysis*. Baltimore: Johns Hopkins University Press for the World Bank, 1983.

Timmer, P. "The Turnip, the New Husbandry, and the English Agricultural Revolution." *Quarterly Journal of Economics* 83, no. 3 (1969): 375–95.

Tocqueville, A. de. *The Ancien Regime and the Revolution*. Trans. Stuart Gilbert. London: Penguin, 2008.

Tordoff, W., ed. *The Politics of Zambia*. Manchester: Manchester University Press, 1974.

Uchendu, V. C. *The Igbo of Southeast Nigeria*. New York: Holt, Rinehart, and Winston, 1965.

Van Bath, R. H. S. *The Agrarian History of Western Europe, 500–1850*. London: Edward Arnold, 1963.

Van Creveld, M. L. *Supplying War: Logistics from Wallenstein to Patton*. Cambridge: Cambridge University Press, 1977.

Varshney, A. *Ethnic Conflict and Civil Life*. New Haven: Yale University Press, 2002.

Velde, F. R., and D. R. Weir. "The Financial Market and Government Debt Policy in France, 1746–1793." *Journal of Economic History* 52, no. 1 (1992): 1–39.

Wasserman, G. *The Politics of Decolonization*. New York: Cambridge University Press, 1976.

Weber, E. *Peasants into Frenchmen*. Stanford: Stanford University Press, 1976.

Weber, M. *Basic Concepts in Sociology*. Secaucus, NJ: Citadel Press, 1985.

——. "Ethnicity." In *Economy and Society*, ed. Guenter Roth and Claus Wittich. Berkeley: University of California Press, 1968.

Weiner, M. *Sons of the Soil: Migration and Ethnic Conflict in India*. Princeton: Princeton University Press, 1978.

Weingast, B. "The Economic Role of Political Institutions." *Journal of Law, Economics, and Organization* 7, no. 1 (1995): 1–31.

Whittaker, D., and J. Goody. "Rural Manufacturing in the Rouergue from Antiquity to the Present: The Examples of Pottery and Cheese." *Comparative Studies in Society and History* 43, no. 2 (2001): 225–45.

Widner, Jennifer. *The Rise of a Party State in Kenya: From "Harembe!" to "Nyayo."* Berkeley: University of California Press, 1992.

Wilkinson, S. I. *Votes and Violence*. New York: Cambridge University Press, 2004.

Willard, J. F. *Parliamentary Taxation of Personal Property, 1290 to 1334*. Cambridge, MA: Medieval Academy of America, 1934.

Wolf, E. R. *Peasant Wars of the Twentieth Century*. New York: Harper and Row, 1969.

Wolf, G. *Becoming Roman: The Origins of Provincial Civilization*. New York: Cambridge University Press, 1998.

Wolff, R. *The Economics of Colonialism: Britain and Kenya: 1870–1930*. New Haven: Yale University Press, 1974.

Woude, A. v. d., A. Hayami, et al. *Urbanization in History: A Process of Dynamic Interactions*. New York: Oxford University Press, 1990.

Wrong, M. *It's Our Turn to Eat*. New York: HarperCollins, 2009.

Young, C. *Politics in the Congo*. Princeton: Princeton University Press, 1965.

Young, M. C. *The Rising Tide of Cultural Pluralism*. Madison: University of Wisconsin Press, 1983.

Zelniker, S. *Changing Patterns of Trade Unionism: The Zambian Case, 1948–1964*. Ann Arbor, MI: University Microfilms, 1981.

INDEX

Acemoglu, D., 12, 125–26
African National Congress (ANC), 79,
    90, 104
agrarian periphery, 124–25
agrarian revolution, 40–43
agrarian societies: characteristics of, 5–
    9, 116–17; ethnicity in, 138; families in,
    6, 8–9, 13, 37, 47, 138; in France and
    England, 37, 39–40, 47–48, 116–18;
    historical comparison using, 5; post-
    imperial nations, 57; power as used
    in, 12, 13, 47; regions as emergent
    property of, 117. *See also* farming
ahoi, 76, 78
Allen, R. O., 157n30
The Anarchy, 22
Anderson, C. W., 13
Angevin dynasty, 3–4, 21, 22; map, 4
Apter, David, 124
Argentina, regional inequality in, 59
athomi, 75, 77
authoritarian regimes, 101, 120, 124

Baldwin, J. W., 30
Barry, J., 105
Bastable, C., 45
Beik, W., 44
Belgium, King Leopold of, 63
Black Prince (Edward of Woodstock),
    35
Brendon, P., 52
Brenner, Robert, 13, 39
Brewer, J., 43
British Empire: uprisings leading to
    downfall of, 78, 86. *See also* empires
    of European nations
Burgundy, House of, 31, 36

Capet, House of, 28, 29–30
Cederman, L.-E., 126
central hierarchy: divergence of France
    and England regarding, 23–24, 31–
    32, 35, 117–18; Huntington on, 12;
    Kaunda and Kenyatta seeking to con-
    solidate hold on, 118–19; medieval
    Church's support for, 20; possibility
    of development and, 23, 134; in
    prisoners' dilemma model, 132, 133,
    134; to replace private control of
    coercion, 11, 14, 18, 20, 23, 132, 134
Central Province, Kenya: Kenyatta's
    death and, 110; as Kenyatta's politi-
    cal base, 88–90, 91, 94, 95, 97, 101,
    105; Mau Mau and, 78, 90. *See also*
    Kiambu district, Kenya
Charles V, 35, 36
Charles VI, 31
Charles VII, 36
Charles VIII, 50
China, growth of middle class in, 116
chivalry, 20
Church in medieval France: peace move-
    ments in, 19–20, 154n22; public wel-
    fare and, 23; royals allied with, 20
civil wars: data on frequency of, 142,
    143–44; economic growth and, 127,
    148, 149–50
coercion: central hierarchy to replace
    private control of, 11, 14, 18, 20, 23,
    132, 134; Kaunda's choice of, 106–7;
    in prisoners' dilemma model, 129,
    130, 132, 134. *See also* violence
Cold War, end of, 111–12
Coleman, D. C., 17
Coleman, James, 124